RELIGIOUS MAXIMS

Having a Connexion with the
Doctrines and Practice of Holiness

by
Thomas C. Upham, DD

Author of
Inward Divine Guidance

SCHMUL PUBLISHING COMPANY
NICHOLASVILLE, KENTUCKY

Published by Schmul Publishing Co.
PO Box 776
Nicholasville, KY USA

Printed in the United States of America

ISBN 10: 0-88019-593-2
ISBN 13: 978-0-88019-593-5

Visit us on the Internet at www.wesleyanbooks.com, or order direct from the publisher by calling 800-772-6657, or by writing to the above address.

Contents

INTRODUCTION 5

PREFACE 7

RELIGIOUS MAXIMS 8

CHRISTIAN HUMILITY 67

CHRISTIAN LOVE 71

PERSONAL FEELINGS 79

RELIGIOUS STANZAS 86

INTRODUCTION

THE NAME OF THOMAS C. Upham is not so well known today, but for a large part of the nineteenth century it was famous thoughout academic and Wesleyan circles.

He was born into a Congregationalist home in 1799, and graduated from Dartmouth College and Andover Theological Seminary, both strongly Calvinist institutions. He pastored the Congregational Church at Rochester, NH, but finally accepted a professor's position at Bowdoin College in Maine. He held the chair for the rest of his professional career.

Regardless of his strong Calvinist indoctrination, Upham became known for his espousal of the doctrine of free will, making it a cornerstone of his groundbreaking work in psychology.

In 1839 his wife, Phebe, was led into holiness by Phoebe Palmer. In December of the same year, she prevailed on her husband to attend the Tuesday Meetings for the Promotion of Holiness at the Palmer home, and by the following February, he was entirely sanctified, himself.

Over the course of subsequent years he wrote a number of articles that were published in *The Guide to Holiness*, along with multiple books. He insisted on the primacy of the human will, freely offered in total subjection to God and his divine will. This surrender results in the sanctifying power of the Holy Spirit, cleansing the soul from inbred sin.

Part of his teaching held that Christians, particularly sanctified believers, would also affect the society around them. He was an active abolitionist, opening his home as a stop on the Underground Railroad for escaping slaves. Harriet Ward Beecher wrote *Uncle Tom's Cabin* while staying in the home of Thomas and Phebe Upham. He became a member of the African Colonization Society, one of several organizations which laid plans to return freed blacks to Africa.

Before he died in 1872, Thomas Upham's influence was broad and deep in the holiness movement, affecting powerful evangelists such as Charles Finney.

PREFACE

THE FOLLOWING MAXIMS do not have relation to religion in its full extent; but to the higher degrees of religious experience. They embody, in a concise and simple form, many of the principles which are laid down and illustrated at some length in the larger treatises on holiness. Tested not more by my own personal experience than by a careful observation of others, they seem to me to be characterized by the truth; but I am not so sanguine as to suppose, that they will all be correctly understood and appreciated by all persons. They must be interpreted and applied, in some degree at least, by the existing mental position. Those, who are truly seeking after holiness of heart, and have realized, in some considerable degree, the object of their search, will not be likely to fail, either in understanding their import, or in making a proper application of them.

—U.

Religious Maxims

I.

FAITH is the continuance, as well as the beginning of the religious life. No man can be justified in Christ, unless he is willing to renounce all merit and hope in himself; and in the exercise of faith receive Christ alone as the propitiation for his sins. No man can experience the grace of sanctification, unless, renouncing all other means of sanctification, all wisdom and all strength of his own, he is willing to receive from God, in the exercise of faith, that wisdom and that strength, moment by moment, without which the sanctification of the heart cannot exist.

II.

Seek holiness rather than consolation. Not that consolation is to be despised, or thought lightly of; but solid and permanent consolation is the result rather than the forerunner of holiness; therefore, he who seeks consolation as a distinct and independent object, will miss it. Seek and possess holiness, and consolation, (not perhaps often in the form of ecstatic and rapturous joys, but rather of solid and delightful peace) will follow, as assuredly as warmth follows the dispensation of the rays of the sun. He who is holy, must be happy.

III.

In whatever you are called upon to do, endeavour to maintain a calm, collected, and prayerful state of mind. Self-recollection is of great importance. "It is good for a man to wait quietly for the salvation of the Lord." He, who is in what may be called a spiritual hurry, or rather who runs without having evidence of being spiritually sent, makes haste to no purpose.

IV.

Be silent when blamed and reproached unjustly, and under such circumstances that the reproachful and injurious person will be likely, under the influence of his own reflections, to discover his error and wrong speedily. Instead of replying, receive the injurious treatment with humility and calmness; and He, in whose name you thus suffer, will reward you with inward consolation, while He sends the sharp arrow of conviction into the heart of your adversary.

V.

Be not disheartened because the eye of the world is constantly and earnestly fixed upon you, to detect your errors and to rejoice in your halting. But rather regard this state of things, trying though it may be, as one of the safeguards which a kind Father has placed around you, to keep alive, in your own bosom, an antagonist spirit of watchfulness, and to prevent those very mistakes and transgressions, which your enemies eagerly anticipate.

VI.

Do not think it strange, when troubles and persecutions come upon you. Rather receive them quietly and thankfully, as coming from a Father's hand. Yea, happy are ye, if, in the exercise of faith, you can look above the earthly instrumentality, above the selfishness and malice of men, to him who has permitted them for your good. Thus persecuted they the Saviour and the prophets.

VII.

"Be ye angry and sin not." The life of our Saviour, as well as the precepts of the apostles, clearly teaches us, that there may be occasions, on which we may have feelings of displeasure, and even of anger, without sin. Sin does not necessarily attach to anger, considered in its nature, but in its degree. Nevertheless, anger seldom exists in fact, without becoming in its measurement inordinate and excessive. Hence it is important to watch against it, lest we be led into transgression. Make it a rule, therefore, never to give any outward expressions to angry feelings (a course which will operate as a powerful check upon their excessive action) until you have made them the subject of reflection and prayer. And thus you may hope to be kept.

VIII.

True peace of mind does not depend, as some seem to suppose, on the external incidents of riches and poverty, of health and sickness, of friendship and enmities. It has no necessary dependence upon society or seclusion; upon dwelling in cities or in the desert; upon the possession of temporal power, or a condition of temporal insignificance and weakness. "The kingdom of God is within you." Let the heart be right, let it be fully united with the will of God, and we shall be entirely contented with those circumstances, in which Providence has seen fit to place us, however unpropitious they may be in a worldly point of view.

He who gains the victory over himself, gains the victory over all his enemies.

IX.

Some persons think of obedience as if it were nothing else, and could be nothing else, than servitude. And it must be admitted that *constrained* obedience is so. He who obeys by compulsion, and not freely, wears a chain upon his spirit which continually frets and torments, while it confines him. But this is not Christian obedience. To obey with the whole heart, in other words, to obey as Christ would have us, is essentially the same as to be perfectly resigned to the will of God; having no will but his. And he must have strange notions of the interior and purified life, who supposes that the obedience, which revolves constantly and joyfully within the limits of the divine will, partakes of the nature of servitude. On the contrary, true obedience, that which has its seat in the affections, and which flows out like the gushing of water, may be said, in a very important sense, to possess not only the nature, but the very essence of freedom.

X.

A sanctified state of heart does not require to be sustained by any mere forms of bodily excitation. It gets above the dominion, at least in a very considerable degree, of the nerves and the senses. It seeks an atmosphere of calmness, of thought, and holy meditation.

XI.

Our spiritual strength will be nearly in proportion to the absence of self-dependence and self-confidence. When we are weak in ourselves, we shall not fail, if we apply to the right source for help, to be found strong in the Lord. Madame Guyon, speaking of certain temptations to which she had been exposed, says, "I then comprehended what power a soul has which is entirely annihilated." This is strong language; but when it is properly understood, it conveys important truth. When we sink in ourselves, we rise in God. When we have no strength in ourselves, we have divine power in Him who can subdue all his adversaries. "The Lord is my rock, and my fortress, and my deliverer; my God, my strength, in whom I will trust; my buckler, and the horn of my salvation, and my high tower."

XII.

In proportion as the heart becomes sanctified, there is a diminished tendency to enthusiasm and fanaticism; and this is undoubtedly one of the leading tests of sanctification. One of the marks of an enthusiastic and fanatical state of mind, is a fiery and unrestrained impetuosity of feeling; a rushing on, sometimes very blindly, as if the world were in danger, or as if the great Creator were not at the helm. It is not only feeling without a due degree of judgment, but, what is the corrupting and fatal trait, it is feeling without a due degree of confidence in God. True holiness reflects the image of God in this respect as well as in others, that it is calm, thoughtful, deliberate, immutable; and how can it be otherwise, since, rejecting its own wisdom and strength, it incorporates into itself the wisdom and strength of the Almighty.

XIII.

The hidden life, which God imparts to his accepted people, may flourish in solitudes and deserts; far from the societies of men and the din and disturbance of cities. From the cave of the hermit, from the cell of the solitary recluse, the fervent prayer has often arisen, which has been acceptable in the sight of God. But it would be a strange and fatal misconception, that religion, even in its most pure and triumphant exaltations, can flourish nowhere else. The home of holiness is in the heart, irrespective of outward situations and alliances; and therefore we may expect to find it, if there are hearts adapted to its reception and growth, in the haunts of business as well as in the silence of retirement; in the palaces of Rome, as well as in the deserts of the Thebais. It is a fatal mistake to suppose that we cannot be holy except on the condition of a situation and circumstances in life such as shall suit ourselves. It is one of the first principles of holiness to leave our times and our places, our going out and our coming in, our wasted and our goodly heritage, entirely with the Lord. Here, O Lord, hast thou placed us, and we will glorify thee here.

XIV.

In the agitations of the present life, beset and perplexed as we are with troubles, how natural it is to seek earnestly some place of rest! and hence it is that we so often reveal our cares and perplexities to our fellow-men, and seek comfort and support from that source. But the sanctified soul, having experienced the uncertainties of all human aids, turns instinctively to the great God; and hiding itself in the presence and protection of the divine existence, it reposes there, as in a strong tower which no enemies can conquer, and as on an everlasting rock which no floods can wash away. It knows the instructive import of that sublime exclamation of the Psalmist, (Ps. lxii. 5.) "My soul, wait thou ONLY upon God; for my expectation is from him."

XV.

Speak not often of your own actions, nor even, when it can be properly avoided, make allusion to yourself, as an agent in transactions which are calculated to attract notice. We do not suppose, as some may be inclined to do, that frequent speaking of our actions is necessarily a proof, although it may furnish a presumption, of inordinate self-love or vanity; but it cannot be denied, that, by such a course, we expose ourselves to temptations and dangers in that direction. It is much safer, and is certainly much more profitable, to speak of what has been done for us and wrought in us; to speak, for instance, of ourselves as the recipients of the goodness of God, than to speak of what we have ourselves done. But even here, also, although it may often be an imperative duty, there is need of deliberation and caution.

XVI.

There are many persons, who would willingly be Christians, and eminent Christians too, if Christianity were limited to great occasions. For such occasions they call forth whatever pious and devotional resources they have, or seem to have, and not only place them in the best light but inspire them, for the time being, with the greatest possible efficiency But on smaller occasions, in the every-day occurrences and events of life, the religious principle is in a state of dormancy; giving no signs of effective vitality and movement. The life of such persons is not like that of the sun, equable, constant, diffusive, and beneficient, though attracting but little notice; but like the eruptive and glaring blaze of volcanoes, which comes forth at remote periods, in company with great thunderings and shakings of the earth; and yet the heart of the people is not made glad by it. Such religion is vain; and its possessors know not what manner of spirit they are of.

XVII.

Out of death springs life. We must die naturally, in order that we may live spiritually. The beautiful flowers spring up from dead seeds; and from the death of those evil principles that spread so diffusively and darkly over the natural heart, springs up the beauty of a new life, the quiet but ravishing bloom of holiness.

XVIII.

A strong faith has the power to make a virtual and present reality of those things which are in fact future. Be it so that we have not the thing itself in the literal sense of the term; that we have not heaven; that we have not the visible presence of Christ; that we have not those things, whatsoever they may be, which constitute the glory and blessedness of the future world. But it is certain that in the Bible we have the promise of them — we have the title deed, the bond, the mortgage, most solemnly made out and delivered to us. All these things are, therefore, ours, if we fully believe in the promise; and they can all be made, in the exercise of entire faith, a virtual and present reality. A man reckons his notes, bonds, and bills, which are the certificates and confirmations of absent possessions, as so much property, as actual money, although it is only virtually and by faith realized to be such. He counts himself as truly and really owning the property, in amount and kind, which the face of his papers, of his notes and bonds, represents; and yet he has nothing in hand but his papers and his faith in the individuals who have signed them. How much more then should we have faith in *our* title-deeds, in *our* bonds and testaments, which are written in the blood of the Son of God, are confirmed by the oath of the Father, and are witnessed by the Holy Ghost! And how much more should we, having such deeds and bonds, and such immutable confirmations of them, count God ours, and Christ and the Holy Spirit ours, and eternal glory ours!

XIX.

It is an excellent saying of the celebrated Fenelon, "It is only imperfection that complains of what is imperfect." It would be well for those who aim at Christian perfection to remember this. Surrounded by those, who constantly exhibit defects of character and conduct, if we yield to a complaining and impatient spirit, we shall mar our own peace, without having the satisfaction of benefitting others. When the mind is in a right position, absorbed in God and truly dead to the world, it will not be troubled by these things. Or if it be otherwise, and we are in fact afflicted, it will be for others and not for ourselves; and we shall be more disposed to pity than to complain.

XX.

Prayer without faith is vain. A pious English writer, one who lived as far back as the days of the Puritans, and who uses various homely but instructive illustrations after the manner of those times, calls prayer "the BUCKET of the soul, by which it draws water out of the wells of salvation; but without faith, you may let down this bucket again and again and never bring up one drop of solid comfort."* It is faith which fills the bucket. And accordingly, if our faith be weak, we shall find but poor and famishing returns. A full bucket depends on the condition of a strong faith.

XXI.

One of the most important requisites of a holy life is PATIENCE; and by this, we do not mean merely a meek and quiet temper, when one is personally assaulted and injured; but a like meekness and quietness of temper in relation to the moral and religious progress of the world. We may be deeply afflicted in view of the desolations of Zion; but let us ever remember and rejoice, that the cause of truth and holiness is lodged safely in the hands of God. With Him a thousand years are as one day; and in the darkest moments when Satan seems to be let loose with ten-fold fury, let us thank God and take courage, because the Lord God Omnipotent reigneth.

---

*Symond's Sight and Faith, printed in 1651.

XXII.

It may sometimes be practically important to make a distinction between a renunciation of the world and a renunciation of ourselves. A man may, in a certain sense and to a certain extent renounce the world, and yet may find himself greatly disappointed in his anticipations of spiritual improvement and benefit. He has indeed renounced the world as it presents itself to us in its externalities; he has renounced its outward attractions; its perverted and idle shows. He may have carried his renouncement so far as to seclude himself entirely from society, and to spend his days in some solitary desert; but it avails nothing or almost nothing, because there is not at the same time an internal renunciation; a crucifixion and renunciation of self. A mere crucifixion of the outward world may still leave a vitality and luxuriance of the selfish principle; but a crucifixion of self necessarily involves the crucifixion, in the Scripture sense, of everything else.

XXIII.

It is one among the pious and valuable maxims, which are ascribed to Francis de Sales: "A judicious silence is always better than truth spoken without charity." The very undertaking to instruct or censure others, implies an assumption of intellectual or moral superiority. It cannot be expected, therefore, that the attempt will be well received, unless it is tempered with a heavenly spirit. "Though I speak with the tongues of men and of angels, and have not CHARITY, I am become as sounding brass or a tinkling cymbal."

XXIV.

We may be deprived of outward consolations, and still have consolations of heart; but this is not all. We may be deprived, in the sovereignty of God, and for wise purposes, of *inward* consolations also; and may be left for a time in a state of mental barrenness and desolation; and yet faith, precious faith, discouraging as this state of things may seem, may still remain; and not feebly merely, but in the strength and fulness of its exercise. It is still our delightful privilege to say of God, that he is *our* God, *our* Father, *our* Friend and portion. "Blessed is the man, that *trusteth* in the Lord."

XXV.

No man ever arrived at Christian perfection, no man ever *can* arrive at that ennobling state, who walks by sight, rather than by faith, and of whom it cannot be said, as of the father of the faithful, "he went out, *not knowing whither he went*." Perhaps we may say, it is the highest attainment of the soul, (certainly it is the foundation of the highest or perfect state in all other Christian attainments,) that of entire and unwavering confidence in God. O, God, we are thine; for ever thine. We will not let thee go, until thou bless us; and when thou dost bless us, still we will not let thee go. For without thee, even blessing would be turned into cursing. Therefore we will ever trust in thee.

XXVI.

Always make it a rule to do every thing which it is proper and a duty to do, in the best manner and to the best of your ability. An imperfect execution of a thing, where we might have done better, is not only unprofitable, but it is a *vicious* execution, or in other words, is morally wrong. He who aims at perfection in great things, but is willing to be imperfect in little things, will find himself essentially an imperfect man. The perfection of the greater will be no compensation, and no excuse for the imperfection of the less. Such a person wants the essential principle of universal obedience. Consider well, therefore, what God, in his providence, would have you perform; and if you feel the spirit of those directions which require us to do all things as unto God rather than unto men, you will not do them with a false heart or a feeble hand. And thus in small things, as well as in great, in those which are unseen, as well as in those which attract notice, it shall be said of you, "Well done, good and faithful servant."

XXVII.

A fixed, inflexible will is a great assistance in a holy life. Satan will suggest a thousand reasons why we should yield a little to the temptations by which we are surrounded; but let us ever stand fast in our purpose. A good degree of decision and tenacity of purpose is of great importance in the ordinary affairs of life. How much more so in the things of religion! He who is easily shaken will find the way of holiness difficult, perhaps impracticable. A double-minded man, he who has no fixedness of purpose, no energy of will, is "unstable in all his ways." Ye, who walk in the narrow way, let your resolution be unalterable. Think of the blessed Saviour. "My God, my God, why hast *Thou* forsaken me?" Though he was momentarily forsaken, at least so far as to be left to anguish inconceivable and unutterable, his heart nevertheless was fixed, and he could still say, "*My* God, *my* God."

XXVIII

We may pray with the intellect without praying with the heart; but we cannot pray with the heart without praying with the intellect. Such are the laws of the mind, that there can be no such thing as praying without a knowledge of the thing we pray for. Let the heart be full, wholly given up to the pursuit of the object; but let your perception of the object be distinct and clear. This will be found honorable to God and beneficial to the soul.

XXIX.

Many persons think they are seeking holiness, when they are in fact seeking the "loaves and fishes." To be holy is to be like Christ, who, as the Captain of our salvation, was made perfect *through suffering*. We must be willing to bear the cross, if we would wear the crown. In seeking holiness, therefore, let us think little of joy, but much of purity; little of ourselves, but much of God; little of our own will, but much of the divine will. We will choose the deepest poverty and affliction, with the will of God, rather than all earthly goods and prosperities without it. It is God we seek, and not happiness. If we have God, he will not fail to take care of us. If we abide in him, even a residence in hell could not harm us. "As the hart panteth after the water-brooks, so panteth my soul after thee, O God. My soul thirsteth for God, for the living God."

XXX.

Thou hast contended with Satan, and hast been successful. Thou hast fought with him, and he has fled from thee. But O, remember his artifices. Do not indulge the belief that his nature is changed. True, indeed, he is now very complacent, and is, perhaps, singing thee some syren song; but he was never more a devil than he is now. He now assaults thee, *by not assaulting thee*; and knows that he shall conquer, when THOU FALLEST ASLEEP.

XXXI.

The value of a thing is known by what it takes to preserve it, as well as by what it originally cost. Men may steal your diamonds, who would not trouble things of less worth. The cost of holiness was the blood of the Son of God; and greatly does he mistake, who supposes that it can be preserved by any thing short of ETERNAL VIGILANCE.

XXXII.

If earthly plants are permitted to spring up in the heart, how is it possible that the tree of holiness should flourish? With the ground already occupied with earthly products, the roots of sanctification, deprived of the nourishment which should sustain them, necessarily wither and die. There is not nutriment enough to sustain both. Hence it is that our Saviour, in his divine wisdom, tells us of those who are choked with the riches, and cares, and pleasures of this life, "and BRING NO FRUIT TO PERFECTION."

XXXIII.

The power of Satan is great; and it is his appropriate business continually to assault the saints of God. If then, in some unhappy and evil moment (by thine own fault be it remembered) he gains an advantage, lament over it deeply, but do not be discouraged. Remember, if the great enemy gets from thee thy *resolution*, thy fixed purpose, he gets all. To be defeated is not wholly to be destroyed; but on the contrary, he, and he only, hath victory written upon his forehead, who, in the moment of severest overthrow, hath still the heart to say, "with the Lord helping me, I WILL TRY AGAIN."

XXXIV.

It seems to have been the doctrine of some advocates of Christian perfection, especially some pious Roman Catholics of former times, that the various propensities and affections, and particularly the bodily appetites, ought to be entirely *eradicated*. But this doctrine, when carried to its full extent, is one of the artifices of Satan, by which the cause of holiness has been greatly injured. It is more difficult to regulate the natural principles than to destroy them; and there is no doubt that the more difficult duty in this case, is the scriptural one. We are not required to eradicate our natural propensities and affections, but to *purify* them. We are not required to cease to be men, but merely to become *holy* men.

XXXV.

It is of the nature of holiness to unite with whatever is like itself. It flies on eagle's wings to meet its own image. Accordingly the soul, so long as it is stained with sin, has an affinity with what is sinful. But when it is purified from iniquity, it ascends boldly upward, and rests, by the impulse of its own being, in the bosom of its God. The element of separation is taken away, and a union, strong, sincere, and lasting, necessarily takes place. *"He that is joined unto the Lord, is one spirit."* 1 Cor. vi. 17.

XXXVI.

It is sometimes the case, that those who are seeking sanctification, anticipate results which are more accordant with human wisdom, than with the ways of divine Providence. They say, "make me clean, and I shall have UNDERSTANDING. Sanctify me, and I shall be made STRONG." Such anticipations, which show that the heart is not yet delivered from its worldliness, are not confirmed, in the sense in which they now exist in the mind, by their subsequent experience. When sanctified, as they are thoroughly emptied of self, they have neither wisdom nor strength of their own. They know not what to do, nor how to do it. They abhor the idea of placing confidence in themselves, and find they must apply to the Saviour for everything. They derive all from him. In the language of Scripture, he is made to them "wisdom, and righteousness, and sanctification, and redemption; that, according as it is written, HE THAT GLORIETH, LET HIM GLORY IN THE LORD."

XXXVII.

It is a melancholy fact, that the religion of many persons is not constantly operative, but is manifested periodically, or at some particular times. It is assumed, for instance, on the Sabbath, but is laid aside on the shelf during the week days; but true holiness, be it remembered, is not a thing to be worn for occasions; to be put off or put on, with an easy accommodation to circumstances, or to one's private convenience. It takes too deep root in the heart to be so easily disposed of as such a course would imply. It is meat, with which we are fed; clothing, with which we are clothed; the interior and permanent principle of life, which animates and sustains the whole man.

XXXVIII.

The remark is somewhere made, and very correctly, that *"it is a great loss to lose an affliction."* Certain it is, that afflictions have great power in purifying the mind; and if it be true that mental purification, in other words, holiness, is a result of all others the most desirable, we may properly attach a great value to whatever tends to this result. Prosperities flatter us with the hope that our rest is here; but afflictions lead our thoughts to another and better land. "Whom the Lord loveth he chasteneth; and scourgeth every son that he receiveth."

XXXIX.

It is a striking remark, ascribed to St. Augustine, that *prayer is the measure of love.* A remark, which implies that those who love much will pray much; and that those who pray much will love much. This remark is not more scripturally than philosophically true. It is the nature of love to lead the person who exercises this passion, as if were, out of himself. His heart is continually attracted toward the beloved object. He naturally and necessarily exercises, in connection with the object of love, the communion of the affections; and this, it will be readily seen, viz. the communion of the affections, is the essential characteristic, and perhaps, it may be said, the essence and sum of prayer. In acceptable prayer the soul goes forth to God in various acts of adoration, supplication, and thanksgiving; all of which imply feelings of trust and confidence, and particularly love to him who is the object of prayer. Accordingly, he who loves much, cannot help praying much; and, on the other hand, when the streams of holy communion with God fail in any considerable degree, it is a sure sign that there is a shallowness and drought in that fountain of love, from which they have their source.

XL.

The divine life, which in every stage of its existence depends upon the presence of the Spirit of God, places a high estimate on mental tranquillity. It is no new thing to remark that the Holy Spirit has no congeniality with, and no pleasure in the soul, where strife and clamor have taken possession. If, therefore, we would have the Holy Spirit with us always, we must avoid and flee, with all the intensity of our being, all inordinate coveting, all envying, malice, and evil speaking, all impatience, jealousy, and anger. Of such a heart, and such only, which is calm as well as pure, partaking something of the self-collected and sublime tranquillity of the divine mind, can it be said, in the truest and highest sense, that it is a TEMPLE FITTED FOR THE INDWELLING OF THE HOLY GHOST.

XLI.

Where there is true Christian perfection, there is always great humility, a Christian grace which it is difficult to define, but which implies at least a quiet and subdued, a meek and forbearing spirit. Whatever may be our supposed gifts and graces, whatever may be our internal pleasures and raptures, they are far from furnishing evidence of completeness of Christian character without humility. It is this grace, which, perhaps more than any other, imparts a beauty and attractiveness to the religious life; and which, while it is blessed with the favour and approbation of God, has the additional efficacy of disarming, in a considerable degree, even the hostility of unholy men. It has the appearance of a contradiction in terms, but is nevertheless true, that he who walks in humility walks in power.

XLII.

It is, perhaps, a common idea, that humility implies weakness; and that lowliness of spirit is the same thing with spiritual imbecility; but this certainly is not a correct view. Christian humility, it is true, has nothing in itself; but it has much in God. In a word, it is the renunciation of our own wisdom, that we may receive wisdom from above; the negation and banishment of our own strength, that we may possess divine strength; the rejection of our own righteousness, that we may receive the righteousness of Christ. How, then, can it possibly be weak and imbecile, while it merely casts off the broken shield of earth, that it may put on the bright panoply of heaven?

XLIII.

In vain does the man attempt to see, whose sight is obscured by the cataract, or by some other equally ruinous disease. Nor is he less blind, over whose spiritual eye sin has drawn its opaque scales and films. Hence it is said in Scripture, "The light shineth in darkness, and the darkness comprehended it not." But break off and purge away the spiritual cataract, and the power of vision will return. In proportion as the eye of the soul is purified from the perplexity of earthly corruptions, does Christ become the true light of the mind; and the beauty of the divine character begins from that moment to unveil itself in all its wonderful perfection. "BLESSED ARE THE PURE IN HEART, FOR THEY SHALL SEE GOD."

XLIV.

Pray earnestly for sanctification. Let this be the desire of your heart from morning till evening, and from evening till morning. On this subject keep the soul resolutely fixed. Take no denial. Refuse to be comforted till you are blessed. But, nevertheless, be careful that you impose no conditions upon God. Say not, Thou must do it in this way or in that. Remember, He is a sovereign, and that you are nothing. Sometimes he comes and turns out the evil legions of the heart with observation and with a triumphant shout. But not unfrequently he is mighty in his silence, and smites and destroys his enemies by an agency so mysterious and secret, that it seems to be alike unseen and unheard.

XLV.

When, on a certain occasion, the pious Fenelon, after having experienced much trouble and persecution from his opposers, was advised by some one to take greater precautions against the artifices and evil designs of men, he made answer in the true spirit of a Christian, MORIAMUR IN SIMPLICITATE NOSTRA, *"let us die in our simplicity."* He that is wholly in Christ, has a oneness and purity of purpose altogether inconsistent with those tricks and subterfuges which are so common among men. He walks in broad day. He goes forth in the light of conscious honesty. He is willing that men and angels should read the very bottom of his heart. He has but one rule. His language is in the ordinary affairs of life, as well as in the duties of religion, "My Father, what wilt thou have me to do?" — This is Christian simplicity; and happy, thrice happy is he who possesses it.

XLVI.

If we wish to rise high in God, we must be willing to sink low in ourselves. It may seen like a contradiction in terms, but it is nevertheless true, that there is no elevation in true religion higher than that of profound humility. He that would be the greatest must become the least. He who was equal with God, condescended to become man; and it was the beloved Son of the Most High that washed the feet of the disciples.

XLVII.

It is not by the mere number of our words and actions, that we can most effectually serve the cause of God and glorify his name. It is the temper in which they are done, rather than the mere multiplication of them, which gives them power. It was the remark of a good man, who had much experience as a minister of the gospel, that *"we mar the work of God by doing it in our own spirit."*

XLVIII.

Many persons seem to be more solicitous for *strong* emotions than for *right* emotions. It would perhaps be a fair representation of their state to say the burden of their prayer is, that their souls might be like "the chariots of Amminadib," or that, like Paul, they may be caught up into the third heavens. They seem desirous, perhaps almost unconsciously to themselves, to experience, or to do, some *great* as well as some *good* thing. Would it not be better for them, in a more chastened and humble temper of mind, to make it the burden and emphasis of their supplication, that they may be meek, forbearing, and forgiving; that they may have a willingness to wash the disciples' feet, and have great love even for their enemies; in a word, that they may bear the image of Christ, who came, not with observation, but was *"meek and lowly of heart?"*

XLIX.

It is quite possible for a man to possess evidence of sanctification, who is temporarily destitute of joyful and rapturous emotions; but it is not possible for man to possess such evidence, who is destitute of a living, operative, and effective conscience. On no part of our nature does sanctification work greater effects than on the conscience. It may be said to give to it an intensity and multiplicity of existence; so that like the flaming sword of the cherubims, it turns every way and guards the tree of life.

L.

The man who is troubled at great sins, particularly such as involve a degree of notoriety, but finds himself slightly affected and troubled in the commission of small or hidden ones, has but little claim to the grace of sanctification. One of the surest marks of sanctification is an increased sensitiveness to sin in all its degrees. The slightest sin is a source of unspeakable misery to the sanctified heart; and gives the soul no rest, till it is washed out in overflowing tears of penitence.

LI.

In a state of mere justification, it is often and perhaps generally the case, that it requires a great mental effort to turn our thoughts and affections from worldly objects, and to fix them, promptly and firmly, upon God. In a state of sanctification, it is the reverse of this. To a holy heart, the difficult and painful effort is to turn away its thoughts and affections from the supreme object of its love, and to fix them, even when duty authorizes it, upon objects of an inferior nature.

LII.

Persons sometimes miss the blessing of sanctification by aiming at it, not being aware of the artifices of the adversary, in what may perhaps be called an unsanctified manner. We are not to desire sanctification, which is probably the case with some, merely because it is an elevated and honorable state of soul, and in point of rank far above any other moral condition, but because it is the only true and worthy consummation of our moral and religious existence, and especially because it is the will of our heavenly Father.

LIII.

All persons are willing to be justified, because all are willing to be saved. But all are not willing to be sanctified, because all are not willing to renounce the pleasures of the world.

LIV.

A spirit of entire obedience is one of the important characteristics of a sanctified state. Not obedience merely, but *entire* obedience. He who obeys in some things, but is fretful and rebellious in others, has not the reality; and it can hardly be said that he has even the appearance of holiness.

LV.

He that is united to God loves solitude; but it is solitude in the relative rather than the absolute sense. True, he is secluded from men; but while he is shut out from the world, he is shut up in God; and in the absence of human society, has the far better society of the Infinite Mind.

LVI.

"*Little love, little trust,*" says Archbishop Leighton. The converse of this is equally true. If there be but little trust, there will be but little love. If we believe the words of our heavenly Father with the whole heart, it will be certain that we shall love him with the whole heart

LVII.

Sanctification consists in LOVE, rather than in KNOWLEDGE. Nevertheless, it is a great and delightful truth, that those who love much, shall know much. They shall be led to the very heights of knowledge. Love shall bring light. The great God himself will be their teacher.

LVIII.

How pleasant, how delightful is a holy imagination! It instinctively refuses and throws away every thing that can defile. It is a sort of inner sanctuary; or perhaps we may call it the bridal chamber of the soul, fitted up and adorned with everything pure in earth and beautiful in heaven; and God himself is the bright light thereof.

LIX.

"Let not your heart be troubled." And in regard to those who indulge the hope that they are sanctified in Christ Jesus, we may well inquire, why should their heart be troubled? Have they not a great protector? Must not the archers first hit Him whom thy soul loveth, before they can hit thee? "What can harm thee," says Archbishop Leighton, who spoke on these things from the fulness of his own pious spirit, "when all must first touch God, within whom thou hast enclosed thyself?"

LX.

It is a great art in the Christian life to LEARN TO BE SILENT. Under oppositions, rebukes, injuries, STILL BE SILENT. It is better to say nothing, than to say it in an excited or an angry manner, even if the occasion should seem to justify a degree of anger. By remaining silent, the mind is enabled to collect itself, and to call upon God in secret aspirations of prayer. And thus you will speak to the honor of your holy profession, as well as to the good of those who have injured you, *when you speak from God.*

LXI.

It is important to make a distinction between sorrow and impatience. We may feel sorrow without sin, but we can never feel impatience without sin. Impatience always involves a want of submission; and he, who is wanting in submission, even in the smallest degree, is not perfect before God.

LXII.

We may lay it down as a principle in the religious life, that everything is wrong, in regard to which we cannot ask the divine direction and blessing. When we sin, we wish, like our first parents, to hide ourselves from Him whom we have offended. But it is the nature of a pure heart always to seek God. Its language is, in all the occurrences and duties of life, "My Father, what wilt *thou* have me to do?"

LXIII.

A Christian is prospectively a citizen of heaven; but actually, and at the present time, he is a citizen of the world. Remember this, and do not think so much of what *is to be* as to forget what *is.* We have a great work in the present life, and in the precise situation where God has placed us. Angels glorify God in heaven; men must glorify him on the earth.

LXIV.

Many profess religion; many, we may charitably hope, possess religion; but few, very few, if we may judge from appearances, are aiming with all their powers at perfection in religion. Nevertheless, it is only upon this last the

Savior looks with unmingled approbation. In regard to all those, who aim at any thing short of bearing his full image, it may be said with truth, that he is wounded in the house of his friends.

LXV.

If we would walk perfectly before God, we must endeavor to do common things, such as are of every day's occurrence, and of but small account in the eyes of the world, in a perfect manner. Some persons are so mentally constituted, that they could more easily undergo the sufferings of martyrdom, than properly regulate and control their feelings in their families during twenty-four hours. How dreadful is that delusion, which excuses itself in its imperfections, because in the providence of God, it is not permitted to do or suffer some great thing. Happy is he, who can do God's will in the solitary place, and who can win the crown without going to the stake.

LXVI.

It is a most dangerous mistake to suppose that we can compensate, by exterior acts, however important they may be, for a want of interior devotion. Men may even minister at the altar, with all the outward eloquence of a Massillon, and yet with hearts full of unbelief. A want of a right or perfect state of the outward action may expose us to the condemnation of men; but an imperfection of the inward or spiritual action exposes us to the condemnation of God. If we can please both God and men, it is well; but above all things, let us not fail to please God, who, in opposition to the course which men usually take, regards the inward principle much more than the mere outward development of it.

LXVII.

If we fail on suitable occasions to declare what God has done for our souls, we shall be likely to offend our heavenly Father. But on the other hand, if we make such declarations, Satan will be likely to be present, and tempt us to spiritual pride. Happy is the man who can relate and extol God's gracious dealings with him, with such meekness and humility, as to furnish no entrance to evil.

LXVIII.

It will help us to ascertain whether we are truly humble, if we inquire whether we are free from the opposites of humility. The opposites of a humble state of mind, (or at least those things which sustain a divergent and antagonist relation,) are impatience, uneasiness, a feeling that something, and perhaps much, depends on ourselves, undue sensitiveness to the praise and the reproofs of men, and censoriousness. No man should account himself truly humbled, who is the subject of these unhappy states of mind.

LXIX.

It is a great practical principle in the religious life, that *a state of suffering furnishes the test of love.* When God is pleased to bestow his favors upon us, when his blessings are repeated every hour, how can we tell whether we love him for what he *is* or for what he *gives*? But when, in seasons of deep and varied afflictions, our heart still clings to him as our only hope and only joy, we may well say, "Thou knowest all things. Thou knowest that I love thee."

LXX.

In believing in the possibility of present sanctification, and in combining with this belief the determination to attain to it, we realize in ourselves the possession of that shield of faith mentioned in the Scriptures, by means of which we are enabled to quench the fiery darts of the adversary. On the contrary, in rejecting this belief, and in acting in accordance with this rejection, we throw away our shield; and it is no more than reasonable to expect that we shall be pierced through and through with the enemy's weapons.

LXXI.

As a general thing, it may be expected that all Christians will find themselves able to bear the GREAT CROSSES of life, because they come with observation; they attract notice by their very magnitude; and by putting the soul on its guard, give it strength to meet them. But happy, thrice happy is he, who can bear the LITTLE CROSSES, which ever lie in wait, and which attack us secretly, and without giving warning, like a thief in the night.

LXXII.

We are told in the Scriptures that all things are the Christian's. Heaven, Christ, God, things present, and things to come, *all* are his. But the possession in the present life is of a two-fold nature—sometimes by present enjoyment, and sometimes by *faith*. More commonly, and undoubtedly for wise reasons, the possession is by faith; but in the view of Him, whose life is hid with Christ, the possession is not on that account any the less sure.

LXXIII.

In endeavoring to estimate the genuineness of our religious experiences, we should ever keep in mind that all those experiences which are wrought by the Spirit of God, and are genuine in their character, tend decidedly and uniformly to personal HUMILITY. "Blessed are the poor in spirit, for theirs is the kingdom of heaven." How can it be otherwise? The tendency of all true religion is to make God everything, and ourselves comparatively nothing; to sink the creature, while it elevates and enthrones the Creator in the centre of the heart. "God resisteth the proud, but giveth grace unto the humble."

LXXIV.

The height and sum of religion is to bear the image of Christ. But can those flatter themselves that they bear the Saviour's image, who are overcome and are rendered impatient by every trifling incident of an adverse nature? O, remember that the life of Christ was from beginning to end a life of trouble. He was often misunderstood and ill-treated by all classes; he was persecuted by the Pharisees; sold by the traitor whom he had chosen as one of his disciples; reviled by the thief on the cross; put to death. But he was far more desirous of the salvation and good of his enemies, than he was of personal exemption from their persecutions. "Father, forgive them; for they know not what they do."

LXXV.

There are various views of Christian perfection, which, on being analyzed, amount to the same thing; and when properly understood, may be regarded as all equally correct. The author of the Imitation of Christ, says, it consists in man's offering up himself "with his whole heart to the will of God; never seeking his own will either in small or great respects, either in time or eternity; but with an equal mind weighing all things in the balance of the sanctuary; *and receiving both prosperity and adversity with continual thanksgiving.*"

LXXVI.

Men bestow honour upon one another. Sometimes they build up, sometimes they pull down. But human opinions cannot alter the reality of things, by making it greater or less than it is. Every man is truly such and such only AS HE IS IN THE SIGHT OF GOD.

LXXVII.

Some persons seem to be able to trust God in everything, excepting in one particular, viz., *they feel that they must do their own fighting*. But what is the language of Scripture? "Dearly beloved, avenge not yourselves. Vengeance is mine, saith the Lord." It is said of Christ himself, Matt. xii. 19, HE SHALL NOT STRIVE.

LXXVIII

When I witness the erroneous estimate which men often place on certain kinds of human knowledge, I am reminded of one of the remarkable sayings which abound in the practical writings of St. Augustine. "Unhappy is he who knows everything else, and does not know God. Happy is he who knows God, though he should be ignorant of everything else."

LXXIX.

There are two classes of Christians; those who live chiefly by emotion, and those who live chiefly by faith. The first class, those who live chiefly by emotion, remind one of ships, that move by the outward impulse of winds operating upon sails. They are often at a dead calm, often out of their course, and sometimes driven back. And it is only when the winds are fair and powerful that they move onward with rapidity. The other class, those who live chiefly by faith, remind one of the magnificent steamers which cross the Atlantic, which are moved by an interior and permanent principle; and which, setting at defiance all ordinary obstacles, advance steadily and swiftly to their destination, through calm and storm, through cloud and sunshine.

LXXX.

There are some heathen philosophers, such as Socrates, Cicero, and Seneca, that occasionally announce moral and religious truths of great value — truths which are susceptible of an interpretation that will bring them into close harmony with the practical doctrines of Christianity. "The fewer things a man wants," said Socrates on a certain occasion, "the nearer he is to God."

LXXXI.

A parent, who loves an obedient and affectionate child, will sometimes give him a picture book, a musical instrument, or some, other thing, as a token of his confidence and love. But if the parent should find the child so much taken up with the picture book as to forget the parental commands, and to be getting into ways of disobedience, he will take it away. And thus God sometimes imparts especial spiritual consolations to his children; but if he finds them, as he sometimes does, more taken up with the joys he gives than they are with himself and his commands, he will remove them. And he does it in great mercy. It is certainly better to lose the gift than to lose the Giver; to lose our consolations, than to lose our God.

LXXXII.

The past is gone; the future has no existence. The PRESENT, which a certain writer calls the "divine moment," or moment of God, is the only period of time which is really committed to us. As there is no other point of time in which we can really serve God but this, which is present to us, the language of the heart should ever be, What wilt thou have me to do know?

LXXXIII.

All deliberate deviation from the will of God necessarily

implies a degree of moral imperfection. If we would be perfect, therefore, our wills must, in the direction of their movement, be completely blended with the will of God. But this does not imply the annihilation of the human will, nor even an obstruction of its appropriate action. It is a correct saying of Francis de Sales, that our "will is never so much enslaved as when we serve our lusts; and never so free as when it is devoted to the will of God."

LXXXIV.

Many who do not love God with the whole heart, nevertheless say that they *desire*, that they *wish* so to love him. O, blinded ones! How can this possibly be, when they are so obviously unwilling to renounce the pursuits and pleasures of the world, by which God is offended and separated from them!

LXXXV.

Often the water that is enclosed in a glass vessel appears to the unaided eye, clear and pure. But if a ray of bright light suddenly strikes the vessel and illuminates it, we at once discover various impurities which had before escaped our notice. So our sins have many hiding places, which conceal them from the natural conscience. And we should ask light from God, a clear, heavenly illumination, that we may find them out.

LXXXVI.

When in the instruction and admonition of others, we have faithfully done our duty, we shall be willing, if we are in a right state of heart, to leave the event, with entire calmness of mind, in the hands of God. We know not what shall profit, whether this or that; but we may be assured, to say the least, that God will do his part, as well as we have done ours, although perhaps in a different way from what we expected. "I have observed," says Bunyan, "that a word cast in by the bye, hath done more execution in a sermon, than all that was spoken besides. Sometimes, also, when I have thought I did no good, then I did the most of all; and at other times, when I thought I should catch them, I have fished for nothing."

LXXXVII.

It is undoubtedly a duty to reprove, on suitable occasions, those who are not perfect before God. But it is sometimes the case that the reproof of others, especially when sharply and frequently uttered, is an evidence of our own imperfection. It too sadly shows, that we have not that spirit of entire self-sacrifice and heart-felt charity which, in the language of the Apostle, "thinketh no evil, but beareth all things, hopeth all things, endureth all things."

LXXXVIII.

If at any time we are injured by others, and find feelings of anger arising in ourselves, we should ever be careful, before attempting to reprove and amend them, to obtain a victory over our own hearts. Otherwise our reproofs, though fully deserved, and although it may be our duty to give them, will be likely to be in vain.

LXXXIX.

We must not only do the right things, but do them in the right manner. The manner of a holy person is generally characterized, as compared with that of others, by a great degree of meekness and quietude, particularly in the ordinary intercourse of life. And this for three reasons. 1. A religious one, viz., that his whole soul rests calmly in the will of God; and therefore, ordinarily, he sees no occasion either for inward or outward perturbation. 2. A philosophical one, viz., an outward perturbation or excitement of manner reacts upon the mind, and sometimes stimulates the inward emotions and passions so much as partially to take them out of our own control, which is injurious. 3. A practical one, viz., a quiet and subdued manner, when flowing from deep religious principle, has an exceedingly impressive and happy effect upon the mass of mankind, especially upon persons of intelligence and cultivation. Still there are some occasions, perhaps not very frequent, when an energy and even violence of manner is not inconsistent with holiness.

XC.

It is a sure sign that our heart is not perfect before God, and does not entirely rest in him, when, like the unconverted Athenians of old, we are anxious to hear or tell some new thing, when we are exceedingly troubled about our own reputation among men, and when in regard to anything of a worldly nature, we exhibit an eager and precipitate state of mind.

XCI.

We are at liberty to take to ourselves the pleasure which naturally results from the use or gratification of the senses, such as eating and drinking, when such use or gratification occurs in the providence of God, and with the divine permission; but if in our thoughts we unnecessarily anticipate such pleasures, or, when they are past, recall them to recollection in a sensual manner, it is a melancholy evidence that God is not the full and satisfying portion of our souls, and that our heart is not wholly right with him.

XCII.

While we admit the duty of ever bearing the cross, we are to remember that we must bear it just where God, in his providential dealings, sees fit to impose it upon us, without assuming the responsibility of either seeking or shunning it. We shall find that God has placed it in the whole course of our life, and at precisely the right place; and all he requires of us is to bear it with a faithful heart when we meet it.

XCIII.

Out advancement in the Christian life may be said to depend upon one thing, viz., whether we wish to direct God, or are willing to resign ourselves TO BE WHOLLY DIRECTED BY HIM.

XCIV.

We may give up all outward things to God; we may surrender houses and lands, wife and children, and whatever else has a worldly value; but unless we give the heart with them, it is after all no real gift. It is a saying of William Penn, in that remarkable book of his, entitled "No Cross, No Crown," that "it is not the sacrifice that recommends the heart; but the heart, that gives the sacrifice acceptance."

XCV.

One of the blessed results of a life of entire religious consecration is, that it necessarily unites us to God. We cannot live, we cannot breathe, we cannot move, even for a moment, in the straight and narrow way, without the divine presence and aid. A half-way Christian is living, or endeavoring to live, in his own strength; but the whole-hearted Christian lives wholly in the strength of God.

XCVI.

It was a saying among the fathers of the Christian church, "NOVIT RECTE TIVERE, QUI NOVIT RECTE OR ARE." In English, "He knows how to live well, who knows how to pray well." And it will always be found, that he who does not live a holy life, either prays amiss, or does not pray at all.

XCVII.

He who serves God perfectly at the PRESENT MOMENT,

though it be in a very small thing, such as the hewing of wood or the drawing of water, does in reality glorify him more than another who is prospectively athirst and anxious for things of much greater consequence, but at the same time neglects or imperfectly performs his *present* duties.

XCVIII.

It is very desirable, that we should always keep ourselves in the order of God's providence; in other words, that we should receive things as they come, and do things as they are presented to us, in the spirit of Christian acquiescence and faithfulness; for that is the only way in which we can truly recognize God as at the helm of affairs, or realize our own nothingness. Let us never forget that God is competent to the direction of his own movements; and that whatever we may think of our own capabilities, he has other agencies in other situations. And what he requires of us, is to be and do just as he would have us, in his own providential time, in his own manner, and his own place.

XCIX.

Everything that exists has its converging point, its elementary principle, its great CENTRE. And when separated from the central tendency, it is necessarily upon a wrong track. The soul, therefore, whose tendencies, are towards the world, can be at most only partially holy. The centre of the sanctified soul is the great God. To that it tends. In that it rests. Neglecting all other attractions, it aims earnestly after the divine mind. It is there, and there only, that it finds a present and everlasting home.

C.

The devil is very skilful in availing himself of particular or especial occasions. He has the sagacity to perceive that it is of no use to throw arrows at the man whose armor is completely on. He therefore keeps himself at a distance, hides himself as it were, says nothing, does nothing. He is waiting to see the shield displaced, or the helmet taken off. And he will be found returning suddenly and powerfully, and too often effectually, when the favorable opportunity presents itself.

CI.

He who keeps his ear open to calumny and backbiting, may reasonably expect to have it filled. The best way, both for our own sake, and that of others, is to keep it shut; to hear but little, and to pray the more.

CII.

It is important to remember that the existence of holiness in the heart does not necessarily alter the manner of action, although it does the principle of action. The farmer and the mechanic plough their fields and smite their anvils as they did before; and if they are estimated by the outward action and the outward appearance merely, they are the same men in many respects as they ever were. But the difference internally, as it reveals itself to the eye of God, who searcheth the heart, is as great as that between sin and holiness, between heaven and hell.

CIII.

Self-contrivances, in other words, calculations made in our own wisdom and strength, and for worldly purposes, are mournful evidences of unbelief and of a heart but partially sanctified. The sanctified heart has learnt the great lesson of a holy cessation from its own plans, and of a humble and patient waiting for the manifestation and forthcoming of the plans of God, that it may have the exceeding blessedness of co-operating with him; moving as he moves; going where he goes; stopping where he stops; knowing that he careth for us; and that our bread and water are safe in his hands. *"He that believeth shall not make haste."*

CIV.

Often amid the duties and distractions of the day, it is impossible for us to visit our usual place of retirement. It is important, therefore, if we would realize the benefits of closet worship when our closets are necessarily closed to us, that we should form the habit of interior retirement and of recollection in God. Can it be doubted, that it is our privilege by means of suitable religious training, accompanied with divine assistance, to remove in a moment every troublesome thought; and retiring inward, to hold communion with God in the secret chamber of the soul? Thus in every place, however disturbed by noise and perplexed by business, we may find a place of inward seclusion, a *spiritual closet*, where God will meet us with his heavenly visitations.

CV.

God is not a God afar off. He is ever present, ever near. But how can he be near us, and not be known? How can he be present, and not be felt? It is because we have blocked up the door of oar hearts with the rubbish of the world. It is because the visitant is more ready than the host. It is he, and he only, who is willing to clear the door of entrance, that will find the divine glory coming in.

CVI.

If, as the wise men of the world assure us, "knowledge is power," the Christian can assert with still greater truth, that *holiness is power*. But holiness wins its victories, not by the accessory aids of cunning devices and of artificial eloquence; but by its own intrinsic excellence. It is gentle in its language, and mild in its gesticulation; but the energy of the great God is heard with transcendent efficacy in its still small voice.

CVII.

There is a remarkable expression of the Saviour, and worthy of serious consideration, viz., "*I can of mine own self do nothing.*" John v. 30. Hence the voice from heaven recognizing the paternal care over him, and saying, "This is my beloved Son, in whom I am well pleased." Hence the interesting statement, that Jesus, who had his weeping infancy and his helpless childhood, "increased in wisdom and stature, and in favour with God and man." Hence the Saviour's disposition to go apart into gardens and forests and mountains, that he might hold communion with God in prayer. Hence, in the mount of transfiguration, the appearance of Moses and Elias, who "spake of his decease, which he should accomplish at Jerusalem." Hence the appearance and the ministration of angels, who appeared to him and administered to him after the temptation in the wilderness and in the agony of the garden. But if the Saviour, in his human nature, was thus dependent on the Father, deriving all things from him and able to do nothing of himself, who among his followers can hesitate for a moment to acknowledge his own littleness and dependence? Who can doubt that whatever religious light and strength he has, comes from God? Who will not rejoice in the "*All of God and nothing of the creature?*"

CVIII.

Amid all the trials of life, amid the rebukes, calumnies, and persecutions of evil men, in seasons when Satan seems to triumph, there is one great consideration which ought to tranquilize and elevate the Christian mind; and that is, that God, who sees the end from the beginning, will glorify himself, and will make even the wrath of his enemies to praise him.

CIX.

Let the time of temptation be the time of silence. Words react upon feelings; and if Satan, in the time of our trials, can induce us to utter a hasty or unadvised word, he will add, by so doing, to the power of his previous assaults, and increase the probability of his getting the victory.

CX.

It is one of the surest signs that the natural life still exists and flourishes in us, if we have what may be called an *outward eye*; and, instead of looking inwardly upon our own failings, are prone closely to watch and to judge others. "Judge not that ye be not judged." One of the first inquiries arising in the mind of a truly humbled and sanctified person, when he sees another in transgression, is, "Who maketh me to differ?" And one of the first supplications which he offers, is, "Lord, have compassion upon my offending brother!"

CXI.

He, whose life is hid with Christ in God, may suffer injustice from the conduct or words of another, but he can *never suffer loss*. He sees the hand of God in everything. He knows that every thing which takes place has either a direct or indirect relation to his present state, and is designed for his benefit. "All things work together for his good."

CXII.

It is impossible for a person to experience a true and deep compassion for sinners, and to be earnestly desirous to rescue them from their state, who does not hate and renounce sin in himself.

CXIII.

He that standeth in God in such a manner as to have no will but the divine will, accounts everything which takes place as a manifestation of God. If God is not the thing itself, God is nevertheless manifested IN the thing. And thus it is with God that he first communicates through the medium of the thing in which he manifests himself. And consequently, as God is the first object which presents itself, he imputes nothing to the subordinate creatures, neither condemning nor approving, neither sorrowing nor rejoicing, without first referring whatever takes place to God, and viewing it in the clearness and truth of the divine light.

CXIV.

It is not safe to dwell upon the failings and weaknesses of the Church, without at the same time dwelling upon the resources and goodness of God. In the exercise of a humble faith we must connect the greatness of the remedy with the virulence of the disease. Otherwise we shall promote the plans of our great enemy by falling into a repining and censorious spirit; a state of mind which is equally injurious to ourselves and offensive to our heavenly Father.

CXV.

It is a sign that our wills are not wholly lost in the will of God, when we are much in the habit of using words which imply election or choice; such as, I want this, or I want that; I hope it will be so and so, or I hope it will be otherwise. When our wills are lost in the will of God, all our specific choices and preferences are merged in God's preference and choice. The soul truly loves the arrangements of God, whatever they may be. In regard to whatever is now, and whatever shall be hereafter, its language is, "Thy will be done."

CXVI.

A holy person often does the same things which are done by an unholy person, and yet the things done in the two cases, though the same in themselves, are infinitely different in their character. The one performs them in the will of God, the other in the will of the creature.

CXVII.

The desires and affections should all converge and meet in the same centre, viz., in the love of God's will and glory. When this is the case, we experience true *simplicity* or *singleness of heart*. The opposite of this, viz., a mixed motive, partly from God and partly from the world, is what is described in the Scriptures as a double mind. The double-minded man, or the man who is not in true simplicity of heart, walks in darkness, and is unstable in all his ways. "If thine eye be SINGLE, thy whole body shall be full of light."

CXVIII.

Confession of sin is an important duty; but there is no true confession of sin where there is not at the same time a turning away from it.

CXIX.

The Scriptures assert the doctrine of a local heaven, and also of a local hell. But it is not the locality or place which constitutes either the one or the other. Supreme love to God is the element or constituting principle of heaven. And nothing more is wanted than its opposite, viz., supreme selfishness, to lay the foundation of all the disorder and misery of hell.

CXX.

When Satan cannot prevent our good deeds, he will sometimes effect his evil objects by inducing us to take an undue and selfish satisfaction in them. So that it is necessary, if we would not convert them into destructive poisons, to be crucified and dead even to our virtues.

CXXI.

No person can be considered as praying in sincerity for a specified object, who does not employ all the appropriate natural means which he can, to secure the object.

CXXII.

The rays of the sun shine upon the dust and mud, but they are not soiled by them. So a holy soul, while it remains holy, may mingle with the vileness of the world, and yet be pure in itself.

CXXIII.

God not only has the disposition to do what is right, but he always does it. Men may have the disposition, and yet fail through physical infirmity, in the realization of the thing; that is to say, in the outward act. *But the disposition is accepted.*

CXXIV.

We often speak of desiring or wishing to be the Lord's; but there is not much ground for supposing that there is any considerable degree of sincerity or strength in such desires, if they stop short of a fixed *determination* or *resolve* to be his.

CXXV.

No person can pray earnestly that the impenitent may be freed from their sins, while he himself knowingly cherishes sin.

CXXVI.

The decisions of the conscience are always based upon

perceptions and acts of the judgment; consequently he who acts from mere desire, without any intervention and helps of the judgment, necessarily acts without the approbation of conscience; and may be said, therefore, in the moral sense of the terms, to act without God.

CXXVII.

God is perfectly tranquil. He is never subject to agitation in any case whatever. And unlikeness to him in this respect, except in what is instinctive and physically unavoidable, indicates the existing state of the mind to be in some respects wrong.

CXXVIII.

Two things, in particular, are to be guarded against in all the variety of their forms, viz., CREATURE LOVE and SELF WILL; in other words, dependence upon self, and dependence upon our fellow men.

CXXIX.

Some portions of the Bible are addressed to the intellect, and some to the heart. The parts addressed exclusively to the intellect, are always understood, where there are corresponding powers and exercises of intellect. The parts addressed to the heart, and which involve truths having relation to the religious affections, can be fully understood only where there are corresponding exercises of the heart. And on this principle, the higher experimental truths of the Bible, such as relate to a full inward salvation, are not likely to be understood and appreciated, except in connection with the experience of such salvation.

CXXX.

To be willing to execute or *do* the will of God, cannot be acceptable to him, unless we are willing, at the same time, to *endure* and *suffer* his will.

CXXXI.

The will of God includes every possible good. He who seeks conformity to the will of God, necessarily seeks whatever is most desirable and best for himself.

CXXXII.

One of those things which particularly characterizes the holy mind, in distinction from the unholy or natural mind, and also in distinction from the partially sanctified mind, is, that in the allotment which falls to it in life, *it chooses to be, and loves to be, where it is*; and has no disposition and no desire to be anywhere else, till the providence of God clearly indicates that the time has come for a removal.

CXXXIII.

Whenever we propose to change our situation in life, by establishing some new relations, or by entering into some new business, it becomes, first of all, a most important religious duty, to lay all our thoughts and plans before our Heavenly Father for his approbation. Otherwise it is possible, and even probable, that we shall be found running the immense risk of moving in our own wisdom and out of God's wisdom, in our own order and out of God's order, for our own ends and out of God's ends.

CXXXIV.

It is one of the marks of a soul wholly given to God, when we find that we are able, viewing all things in God and God in all things, to receive both praise and blame with a quiet and equal spirit; neither unduly depressed on the one hand, nor elated on the other.

CXXXV.

It is good to take up and to bear the cross, whatever it may be, which God sees fit to impose. But it is not good and not safe to make crosses of our own; and, by an act of our own choice, to impose upon ourselves burdens which God does not require, and does not authorize. Such a course always implies either a faith too weak or a will too strong; either a fear to trust God's way, or a desire to have our own way.

CXXXVI.

The more we are disunited from the unnecessary and tangling alliances of this life, the more fully and freely will our minds be directed to the life which is to come. The more we are separated from that which is temporal, the more closely shall we be allied to that which is eternal; the more we are disunited from the creatures, the more we shall be united to the Creator.

CXXXVII.

Adversity, in the state of things in the present life, has far less danger for us than prosperity. Both, when received in the proper spirit, may tend to our spiritual advancement. But the tendency of adversity, in itself considered, is to show us our weakness, and to lead us to God; while the natural tendency of prosperity, separate from the correctives and the directions of divine grace, is to inspire us with self-confidence, and to turn us away from God.

CXXXVIII.

The goods of this world, those things which are suited to our convenience and comfort, are not necessarily unholy. Unholiness attaches to the manner; that is to say, to the spirit or temper, considered in relation to God, in which we receive and hold and employ them. If we receive and hold them as God's gifts, and in subordination to his will, they are good. But if we hold and employ them as our own possessions, and irrespective of God's will, they are evil.

CXXXIX.

It is as necessary, in the progress and support of a holy life, to regulate our friendships and our love, (we mean here our love of creatures,) as it is to regulate our displeasure and anger. We may as really love too much and sin, as we may be displeased too much and sin. The holy mind may be said, with a degree of propriety, to stand in a state of indifference, relatively to *itself*. That is to say, it seeks nothing, desires nothing, loves nothing, is averse from nothing, and is angry with nothing, except in God's time and way, IN God and FOR God.

CXL.

As Christians, who aim at the highest results of Christian experience, attach a suitable value to your reputation; to that honourable acceptance and name which God may see fit to give to you with your fellow men; but do not seek it in the first instance, nor seek to maintain it afterwards by any other means than those which God approves. As no other name is desirable, except what he in his providence gives, so no other name is desirable except what he is able and willing to keep for us. In other words, trust your reputation with God in the same way and on the same principles that you trust every thing else with him.

CXLI.

It is a principle in sound morals, and equally so in religion, that actions should be judged of by the intentions which prompt, rather than by the success which attends them. Our great work, therefore, is to have a right heart.

CXLII.

It is very important that our desires should be kept in entire subjection. If the providence of God reaches to all things, not excepting the numbering of the hairs of our heads, it is certain that a man never desires strongly without running the hazard, which is always a very great and responsible one, of exercising desire against the claims of God's providential order. We cannot keep in harmony with God, without having out desires in subjection to a higher desire or purpose, that of God himself.

CXLIII.

It is the providences of God, taken undoubtedly in connection with other sources of information, which indicate, in particular, the will of God; and those providences are revealed, and can be revealed, only *moment by moment.* The doctrine of living in the present moment, therefore, or in the state of momentary inward recollection, is founded not only on the necessity of watching against temptation, which is one reason for it, but on the fixed and immutable relation existing between the providences of God and the claims of God upon the human soul. If we are bound to obey the will of God, and if we can know his present will, which is necessarily the source of present obligation, only in connection with his providences, it is very obvious that there can be no other mode of holy living than that of living by the moment.

CXLIV.

In the discharge of those duties which are incumbent upon us, if our hearts are right with God, we shall consider it indispensably necessary to employ just means, as well as to aim at just ends. And however just and desirable the ends may be, in themselves considered, if the methods or means are such as we cannot rightfully employ, we must always regard the end as forbidden.

CXLV.

"The kingdom of God is within you." The soul's inward redemption, that is to say, its redemption from present sin,

and its unity with God in will and life, can be sustained, and sustained only, by the present indwelling and operation of the Holy Ghost.

CXLVI.

The world is sometimes described as a troublesome world; but there is still greater and more practical truth in a remark which is sometimes made, that our chief troubles do not arise from our living in the world, *but from the fact of the world's living in us.*

CXLVII

It is difficult to attach too much importance to the present moment, considered in its relations to inward experience. The value of our past experience, in itself considered, can never be changed; and the untried future is wholly unknown to us. It is obvious, therefore, that we are what we are NOW. We are, and we can be, only what we are, when we are estimated by the facts, the relations, and the duties of the present moment. It is only in the facts, the relations, and the duties of the present moment that God offers himself to our notice. We must meet with him there, and harmonize with him there, or meet with him and harmonize with him nowhere.

CXLVIII.

Happiness can be found only in being resigned and contented in the Divine Order. That is to say, in being resigned and contented in that situation, whatever it may be, in which God's providential order has evidently placed us. If the angels in heaven, like men under the influence of the natural life, were constantly desiring to change their position, and to assume the place of archangels or other higher beings, they would exhibit a spirit which would be displeasing to God, and which could not fail to render them unhappy.

CXLIX.

There are various relations running through the different kinds and degrees of faith, which are worthy of notice. For instance, we must have a belief, that God is, and that he is the rewarder of those who diligently seek him, before we can believe in him as accepting us. And again, we must believe in him as granting forgiveness and acceptance to ourselves, and consequently as sustaining to us the relation of a Father and a friend, before we can have faith to make known to him our requests to him in the behalf of others.

CL.

It implies great grace to remain, for any considerable length of time, in religious solitude, and in the performance of private religious duties. But it implies equally great and perhaps greater grace, to enter into society and to mingle in human conversations in a proper religious spirit. If it were otherwise, why is it so common for religious men to prepare for the special hazards of society, by first seeking religious strength in retirement?

CLI.

What is done hastily, is not likely to be done well. There is need, therefore, of HOLY DELIBERATION; especially when we consider, that the results of an eternity may depend on the movements of a single moment.

CLII.

When we are injured and afflicted by our fellow-men, we should remember, that our heavenly Father felt the wound *first*. He always feels in what his people feel, and if, for wise purposes, he is patient, and bears with the infliction, whatever it may be, we should both be taught and be encouraged to do likewise.

CLIII.

Our Heavenly Father takes an interest in all the works of his hands. He beholds the reflection of his own wisdom in every blade of grass, in every flower of the desert, in every waterfall. There is no living thing in the earth, the air, or the waters, over which God does not watch with a Father's love. Those who bear God's image, in being possessed of a holy heart, not only connect God with all his works, but sympathize with him in his deep interest for everything he has made.

CLIV.

God, in the formation of his spiritual work, can stamp no image and form no feature, but the image and the feature which exists eternally in himself. And accordingly, all holy souls are not only lights in the world; but being born of God and bearing his image, are necessarily mirrors of the Divinity. If the mirror is clear, God is manifest. And just in proportion, as it is stained and soiled, there is no divine reflection. God is no longer a subject of inward consciousness, nor of outward observation.

CLV.

In the early periods of our religious experience, we are chiefly interested in what Christ was by SITUATION, his birth in the manger, the incidents of his childhood, his temptations and labours, his betrayal and his crucifixion. At a later period, we are interested, in a still higher degree, in what Christ was and is by CHARACTER, his purity, his condescension, his forbearance, his readiness to do and suffer his Father's will, his love. The first method of contemplating Christ is profitable; the second still more so. The tendency of the one is to lead to a Christ outward, to Christ of the times of Herod and of Pilate, to a Christ with blood-stained feet and with a crown of thorns; who is now gone, and who never can exist again, as he was then. The tendency of the other is to lead us to a Christ inward; who lives unchanged in his unity and likeness with his Father; for ever the same in himself, and for ever the same in the hearts of those who are born in his image. Christ outward, is precious, and always will be precious, historically; "THE STAR OF MEMORY." Christ inward, who can never die, and who reproduces himself in the hearts of his followers, is still more precious, by present realization; *the star, the sun of the affections.*

CLVI.

God is not only in the beginning and the end; but in all the intermediate methods and instrumentalities which connect them together. He who lifts a finger or moves a foot in any enterprise without God, does it at the hazard, not only of displeasing God, but of failing of his object. We ought, therefore, to exercise the same sense of dependence, and the same submissiveness of spirit, in the choice and employment of the means applicable to a given end, which we exercise in relation to the end, when in the providence of God it is either accomplished or fails to be accomplished. *"Except the Lord build the house, they labor in vain that build it. Except the Lord keep the city, the watchman waketh but in vain."* Ps. cxxvii. 1.

CLVII.

The Holy Spirit does not teach by arbitrary acts, or those acts which have no relation to the constitution of the human mind; but by silently, and yet effectually, inspiring and guiding the movements of the natural powers of perception and knowledge, in *co-operation with their own action.* "Strive, therefore, to enter in." He who desires and purposes to be holy, must employ the appropriate means to be holy. He must be willing to think and to reason; he must be willing to reflect, to resolve, to pray; doing all, however, under the guidance of the great inward Teacher, who gives life without countenancing inactivity, who is the inspirer of human movement, but is not the substitute for it.

CLVIII.

It is one part of the office of the Holy Spirit to illuminate the intellect, and through the intellect to impart clearness and strength to the conscience. We ought, therefore, highly to value not only those affections, which are originated and strengthened by the Holy Spirit, but also an intellect and conscience, enlightened from the same source. Especially when we consider, that a spiritually enlightened conscience is the surest guide in relation to the true character and the right degree of the affections.

CLIX.

If an intellect and conscience, enlightened by the Holy Spirit, furnish the instrumentality, which indicates the nature and regulates the degree of the religious affections, then the law of religious experience requires us to *know* the right, as well as to be and do the right. Be not contented, therefore, to remain in ignorance. Sit at the feet of the great Teacher, and *learn*. "For this cause," says the Saviour, " came I into the world, that I should bear witness unto the TRUTH." And again he says in another place, "The TRUTH shall make you FREE." John viii. 32, xviii. 37.

CLX.

He who can say from a full and sincere heart, THY WILL BE DONE, is in a state of continual prayer. And it is a prayer, which, although it is general in its form, may be regarded as realizing and including in itself all particular and specific prayer. He, who is the subject of it, sympathizing, as he does with the divine mind, prays for everything which

God requires him to pray for. He can as really pray for all the objects of prayer without specifically knowing them, as he can adore all the purposes of God without knowing them. There is no sinner in all lands, and no sorrow in the wide world, which he does not virtually and at the same time really present before God. It should be remembered, however, that this sublime state of mind, which exists much less frequently than it should do, is entirely consistent with specific prayer, and that it really lays the best foundation for it.

CLXI.

Nothing can be properly called small, which really offends God; because the offence is to be estimated not only by the occasion, however small it may be, on which it takes place, but especially and chiefly by its relation to a Being of infinite wisdom, goodness, and holiness.

CLXII.

He who hates crime, or any kind of wrong- doing because wrong-doing is hateful in itself, does well; but he who, on analyzing his feelings, finds that he hates it through fear of its punishment, rather than from aversion to its nature, cannot with any good reason be said to hate it at all.

CLXIII.

It is an easy thing for the holy soul, however high the state of its advancement, to separate itself from the condition of present acceptance and communion. Nothing more is wanted to bring about this deplorable result, than the least intentional neglect, the least known and deliberate infidelity.

CLXIV.

Nature bleeds, when our reputation suffers from the evil

opinions of our fellow-men; but the true and only infallible balm for this wound is the consciousness that we have done those things, for which our fellow-men blame and distrust us, with a single eye to the divine glory.

CLXV.

If we wish for practical religious wisdom, we must find it where we are, that is to say, at the present time, and in the present place; because it is the present time and the present place which furnish us with the facts of God's providence, independently of which it is impossible for us to form a correct estimate of truth and duty.

CLXVI.

The soul is not happy, which is not at rest. But the soul can never have true rest, which places its confidence in anything short of God. Mutability and uncertainty are characteristics of everything which has not God in it.

CLXVII.

When God has fully prepared the heart for religious action, we need not fear that he will fail to find for us our appropriate work. He knows the work which is to be done, and the time of its being done, as well as the dispositions, which are fitted for doing it. Be watchful, therefore, but wait also. A good soldier, in the spirit of watchfulness, is always ready for action; but he never anticipates, by a restless and unwise hurry of spirits, the orders of his commander.

CLXVIII.

It is the part of a Christian, especially of a soul truly devoted and holy, to do good to others. But we should always remember, that we shall lose the grace which God has imparted, and shall bring barrenness and darkness into our own hearts, when we seek to do good to others, without a suitable sense of our personal dependence, and without a humble and watchful regard to the order of the divine providences.

CLXIX.

"Forgive us our trespasses, as we forgive those that trespass against us." If we rightly understand these and other passages of similar import, no person can regard himself as accepted of God, who has not the spirit of forgiveness towards his neighbor.

CLXX.

Holiness is but another name for love. But that love which constitutes the essence of holiness, is a love, which by its very nature conforms itself to the truth. It loves only that which ought to be loved; and it loves, not in defect or excess, not periodically and violently, but precisely according to the truth.

CLXXI.

That love, which is not according to the truth, when the truth is capable of being known, in other words, that love, which is not precisely conformed to its object, will always be found to be vitiated by some human imperfection; by unwarrantable indolence, or by interested fear, or by selfish complaisance.

CLXXII.

The providence of God includes not only events but dispositions. In other words, there are moral providences as well as natural providences. God knows the tempers of men; the feelings, whether good or evil, which predominate in their hearts. And whether they shall exhibit those tempers at one time rather than another, on one occasion rather than another, is a matter which is left hidden in the divine providences alone.

CLXXIII.

If our neighbour injures us by improper words or in any other way, it is as much an event in divine providence, considered in its relation to ourselves, as any event could be, by which we might be afflicted. God's hand is really in it, although it may require a higher faith to see it. Happy is the man who has the requisite faith, and who has those patient and acquiescent dispositions, which such a faith is calculated to produce.

CLXXIV.

Afflictions are from the same benevolent source from which mercies originate. They equally indicate God's goodness, and in their result will show that they are equally beneficial, and perhaps more so, to those who, in being the subjects of them, receive them in a proper temper of mind.

CLXXV.

Seasons of retirement and of private communion with God, are of great value; but they ought never to be sought and indulged in, at the expense of those more social and public duties to which the providence of God clearly calls us. Such a course, which could originate only in the reality of selfishness under the appearance of sincere devotion, would be a violation of God's will, and would be exceedingly injurious.

CLXXVI.

There are few situations more trying than those in which we find our labours for the spiritual good of others fruitless. It requires strong faith, especially in ministers of the gospel, not to find the yoke of God's providence, which binds us to such a situation, a heavy one. Nevertheless it is possible, that the duty which we owe to our Heavenly Father requires us to stay there with the same submission and the same grateful confidence, which reconcile us to other trying circumstances.

CLXXVII.

It is sometimes a serious and important question with the Christian, whether he is in his right position, standing precisely where he should stand, in the order of God's providence. In order to understand what we ought to do under such circumstances, we should be faithful, in the first place, to every obligation which our present situation imposes; so that there shall be found within us no condemnations and rebukes of conscience for neglect of duty. And discharging our duties in this manner, we should remain calmly and quietly where we are, till the providences of God shall so clearly open another situation, that conscience, enlightened by the Holy Ghost, (as the conscience of a truly consecrated man always is,) shall condemn us for not leaving the present one.

CLXXVIII.

Human friendships, resting on the changeable foundation of humanity, cannot be more stable, more enduring, than the frail foundation which supports them. They exist to-day; and too often are dissolved and scattered to-morrow. But he, who on Christian principles possesses God's friendship, will never find him changing and different in future from what he is at present. He is a friend to-day, to-morrow, and for ever.

CLXXIX.

Indifference to religion is a great evil. Indifference to SELF, (that is to say, indifference to our own interests considered *as separate from those of God*,) is a great good. Such is the nature of the human mind, that we cannot be indifferent to everything. To say, therefore, that we are indifferent to ourselves, if we properly recognize and feel the relations we sustain, and if we say it in a Christian spirit, is essentially the same thing as to say, that we possess a heart truly given to God. Self is forgotten, in order that God may be remembered; SELF is crucified in order that God may live in the soul.

CLXXX.

To the holy mind the faults and backslidings of the followers of Christ furnish occasions of humiliation and prayer; but never of secret complacency and of ungenerous triumph. While, therefore, the errors of Christians are deeply to be lamented, they are never, except when truth and holiness clearly require it, to be published abroad. *"Whatsoever ye would that men should do unto you, do ye even so to them; for this is the law and the prophets."*

CLXXXI.

There are different kinds of sorrow. There is a godly sorrow, and a worldly sorrow; a sorrow which works life, and a sorrow which works death. The one is the product of man's unsanctified nature; the other is inspired by the Holy Ghost. The one is the companion of self-seeking, envy, and avarice; the other is the associate of humility, of love of the truth, and of desires after holiness. The one is sorrow, because we have offended God; the other is sorrow because we have not gained the world.

CLXXXII.

Nothing exists, which does not have its principle of existence. And accordingly, that can never be manifested outwardly, which does not exist inwardly in its principle of existence. And hence, it is not unreasonable to say, that God must dwell in the soul, before God can be manifested in the life. And hence it is said of the Christian, who keeps the divine commandments, "My Father will love him, and we will come unto him, *and make our abode with him."* And again it is said, *"Ye are the temple of the living God."* John xiv. 23; 2 Cor. vi. 16.

CHRISTIAN HUMILITY

SOME OF THE MARKS OF TRUE HUMILITY.

ONE of the surest evidences of sanctification of heart is true humility. It is this state of mind, when viewed in its true aspect, to which the Saviour seems to have especial reference, when he represents to his followers the importance of becoming *like little children*. Without proposing, at this time, to enter very fully into this subject, we shall proceed to mention some of the marks or characteristics by which true humility is known.

I. — The truly humble man does not desire great things for himself; nor does he desire great things in any worldly sense whatever. If God has given him distinguished talents, he is thankful for it. If God has placed him in a position of great influence in the world he is thankful for it. But he can be happy in his talents, in his influence, and any other possession which the world deems valuable, only as they are the gifts of God, and as they are employed for the promotion of his glory. If God sees fit to deprive him of knowledge, property, influence, or any other mere earthly good, he is equally thankful, equally happy; so that he does not desire worldly prosperity in itself considered; and not desiring it, the possession of it does not puff him up with sentiments of pride.

II.—Deeply sensible of his entire weakness, dependence and unworthiness, it is entirely natural to him to seek and to take the lowest place. It does not occur to him, (certainly not as a matter of cherished and pleasing reflection,) that a more conspicuous position would be appropriate to him. But if the indications of the providence of God should call him to a higher place, and impose upon him duties of a more elevated and conspicuous character, he does not refuse them. True lowliness of spirit leads him to feel that it would be very unsuitable for him to distrust the wisdom of God, and to take the direction of himself into his own hands; so that the same humility which, in ordinary cases, leads him to decline places of responsibility and notoriety, leads him also to submit himself without hesitation to the guidance of providence, and of the divine will. It should always be remembered, therefore that the truly humble man, who has a profound sense of his own nothingness, and always feels at home in the lowest place, nevertheless realizes that he can do all things through the wisdom of God guiding him, and the grace of God strengthening him. It does not follow, because true humility is distrustful of itself, that it is distrustful of God.

III.—The truly humble man is not troubled and afflicted, because in some respects he fails in securing to himself the good opinion of his fellow men. It is true, he attaches a degree of value to the favorable sentiments of others; but as he attaches unspeakably greater value to the favour of God, he can meet their opposition, their rebukes and misrepresentations, with entire calmness and peace of spirit. And hence it is that, in ordinary cases, when he is the subject of such misrepresentation and abuse, he is not particularly solicitous to defend himself, and to make replies. I mean to say, that he does not discover anxiety and trouble of mind in relation to it. He knows, if he acts in simplicity of heart and with a sincere desire for the divine glory, God will so order events that in due time the honour of his reputation will be sustained. So that he is willing, for the present at least, to stand silent in the presence of his accusers, that both he and they may see the salvation of the Lord.

IV.—The man who is truly humble, is not troubled and "disquieted at those unavoidable imperfections which exist in his own person and mind. It is very true that he sometimes mourns over them, as the indications and sad results of our fallen condition; but so far as they cannot be corrected, so far as they are really unavoidable, he submits to them, however painful they may be, as facts and incidents in his condition and being, which originate in the wise dispensations of an unsearchable Providence. It is true, he is thus cut off from many ways or forms of usefulness; but, though afflicted, he does not allow himself to be disquieted. He is aided in thus maintaining himself in interior rest, by the important consideration that God, when he sends intellectual or bodily imperfections and weaknesses, and thus renders a person apparently useless, can avail himself of other instrumentalities and operate in other ways."*

V.—The truly humble man, although he is not destitute of that observation and judgment which are necessary to discriminate between right and wrong, is disposed to look with a forbearing and pitying eye on the faults of others. If a brother falls into transgression, while he himself is preserved, he knows who it is, and who *alone* it is, that makes him to differ. He feels deeply that he himself would be no better than others that fall into errors and sin, if he should cease to be sustained by the special grace of God. And he cannot fail, therefore, to remember that blessed passage of Scripture, which has a close connection with the highest

*See the Life of Faith, Pt. II. Chap. 12.

experiences in religion: *"Judge not, that ye be not judged."*

VI. — The truly humble man receives with great meekness of spirit all adverse occurrences — all sudden injuries of body and estate — all disruption of social ties by death or in other ways, and whatever other forms of human affliction exist. Whatever comes upon him, he feels that he deserves it. He opens not his mouth; he stands dumb, as the sheep before its shearer. Satan, it is true, tempts him to evil thoughts; but he resists them easily and triumphantly. It seems to him a light thing to suffer anything which God sees fit to impose. He bears the cross like one that loves it.

In connection with these traits of feeling, which obviously characterize the humble man, we may perceive more clearly and definitely in what true humility consists. It is obvious that it does not consist, as some might perhaps suppose, in mere sorrow. It is well known that sorrow sometimes exists in combination with impatience or with pride; but true humility excludes both of these. Nor does it consist in mere depression of spirits; a state of feeling which, it must be admitted, sometimes imparts an outward appearance of humility. But, in reality, the two states of mind are far from being identical. Humility consists in those feelings, whatever they may be, which are appropriate to a realizing sense of our entire dependence upon God. In other words, it consists in a deep sense of our own nothingness, attended with an equally deep and thorough conviction, that God is, and ought to be, to every holy being, the ALL IN ALL.

CHRISTIAN LOVE

OF THE LAWS OF LOVE AS IT EXISTS IN THE SOUL WHICH IS WHOLLY GIVEN TO GOD

CHRISTIANITY, when fully developed in the heart, is a life;—that is to say, it is a living principle which operates of itself. And this principle is pure or holy LOVE. Now, if love in holy men has life in itself, just as holy love has in the divine mind, then it must have a mode, form, or law of life. For life, or a true living principle, without some mode or form of life, in accordance with which it developes itself, would be an impossibility.

Hence a question arises of no small interest, viz., What are those forms or laws, in accordance with which the development of holy love takes place?

(1.) Love, in its basis or elementary form, is the desire of the happiness of others. Its first law, therefore, (a law which is involved in its own nature,) is, that it desires the happiness of all beings, in every degree of existence, which are capable of happiness. Love (we mean, of course, pure or holy love,) may exist *latent* in the mind; but it can never be brought to development, and exist in exercise, except in connection with the presence of some object, which is capable of being loved. And when such object is present, it cannot help loving it in the sense of desiring its happiness. Such is the fundamental law of love — a law which is so essential to it, that it may be described as a part of its own nature.

(2.) A second law of love is, that it will flow out to beings who are capable of being loved, other things being equal, *in a degree proportioned to that capability;* — in other words, in a degree proportioned to the amount or extent of their physical existence. We naturally feel, for instance, more benevolent sympathy with a man or angel, than we do with a worm or an insect, because the former have greater expansion or extent of being; and therefore being susceptible of higher degrees of suffering or enjoyment, they are the natural and appropriate objects of higher degrees of love. This law is as strict and invariable as the first; and is a part of love's nature.

(3.) A third law of love is, that, other things being equal, it will flow out to beings who are capable of being loved, in a degree proportioned to the degree of their moral excellence; in other words, in a degree proportioned to the development of love, of which they themselves are the subjects. If by our nature we desire the good or happiness of a being, we naturally and necessarily love such a being the more, if we perceive it to be a source of good and happiness to others, which is the case with all morally good or holy beings.

(4.) From the combined action of the two last mentioned laws, it will follow, that God is the object of the supreme or highest love. God is at the same time the infinity of natural existence, and the infinity of moral perfection; so that realizing in himself those attributes of existence and character, which attract the highest degree of love, he of right ought to be loved, and in point of fact will be loved, by all holy beings "with all their soul, and mind, and strength."

(5.) Love, when existing in perfect purity, will by its own living power dispense itself to beings inferior to God, in accordance with the preceding complex law—namely, flowing out to each one in its appropriate place, in a degree corresponding with the extent or greatness of its being, combined with its moral excellence. So that the holy soul, under the influence of this law, naturally loves God in God's degree; loves angels in the angelic degree; and loves men in the human degree.

(6.) And these more general laws of love are modified by another. That is to say, we are to take into view, not only being and character, but *relative situation*. Holy love, other things being equal, will, by its own law of action, love most those beings who are brought into the *nearest relations with it*. The same being is a more appropriate object of some degrees and forms of love, in some situations, than he would be in others. And therefore it is natural to suppose that he will be loved more in such situations. Accordingly a man, whose heart is the subject of holy love, will love a parent or child, a brother or sister, and other members of his family, more than others; because, in consequence of their situation, and the relations they sustain, they are the appropriate objects of such higher love. It is impossible, in the nature of things, that the same amount of love should be practically bestowed upon others, who sustain less intimate relations. The fact of less intimacy of relations implies, that the channels of love are not so fully open in those directions; and therefore it is impossible that an equal degree of love should flow out.

And I would add a remark further in connection with what has been said. Holy love, being a living and permanent principle, is not brought into exercise as a matter of mere prudential calculation, or as the result of a mere effort of the will. If it were will work, it would be man's work;

but being God's work, it has a permanent nature. Requiring only its appropriate object, it acts naturally; and of course without labour or effort of any kind; turning instinctively from what is evil; harmonizing with what is good; moving always in its appropriate sphere, under the regulation of its divine relationships, correspondences, and impulses; and as steadily and easily as planets move in their courses, and as descending rivers flow to the ocean. Blessed are those who know what this is from experience.

But we pass now to another view of the subject. Holy love, considered *as a permanent life in the soul,* twofold, EMANATIVE and ATTRACTIVE. And both forms or methods of operation are regulated by fixed laws. Love, in its EMANATIVE nature, goes forth, as it were instinctively, and without thinking of its own happiness, to seek the happiness of others. And it flows out to them, not accidentally, not independently of all regulation; but in accordance with fixed principles—principles which have relation to time and place, to extent and characteristics of being. It is the form of the life of love, which I have just explained.

But holy love presents another aspect, and may indeed be said to possess another nature—a nature which the world has known *hitherto but very imperfectly,* because its eye has not been opened to behold and admire it. I refer to its attribute of ATTRACTION—an attribute, which, though scarcely known, is a real and inherent part of true love, and which is destined, under favourable circumstances, to exert a mighty influence.

Love, in its *attractive* nature, has the power of drawing the thoughts and affections of holy beings to itself. This power it does not seek; but it possesses it without seeking. The beneficence of its emanative nature, the brightness, as it were, of its outgoing, lays the foundation of that remarkable power which it has of drawing the eyes of all beings to the contemplation of its own light.

And of this I propose to give a little further explanation.

Of all things or objects of contemplation, either in the natural or moral world, holy love is the most beautiful. So that it should ever be remembered, that love is not more love than it is *beauty;* and it can cease to be the one, as soon as it can cease to be the other. Beauty, by the order and the necessary nature of things, is the grace, the radiance, the light of love. And love possesses the remarkable trait of its attractive power through the medium of its beauty;—it being the characteristic of beauty to pleasure. Love could not be *known* as beauty, even if it could *exist* as such, if it failed to give pleasure. And it is the characteristic or attribute of that which gives pleasure, to *exert a propitiative and attractive power towards itself.*

To give pleasure, and to *attract* through the medium of that pleasure, is an attribute even of *natural* beauty. The flower by the way side arrests the notice of the traveller; we gaze with delight upon the extended and variegated forest; the eyes turn, instinctively as it were, upon the stars in their bright and quiet motion, because there is something even in natural beauty, which appeals to, and which controls the heart. But *moral* beauty—that beauty which attaches itself to *virtue*—is of a much higher kind, and has much more of attractive power than mere natural beauty. But virtue, when not considered abstractly, but as a *principle in living exercise,* is the same as holy love.

Adopting, therefore, this conclusion, that love, by its own nature, has an *attractive* as well as an emanative power—that it not only goes forth to do others good, but attracts others to itself by its own goodness, we proceed now to say, that the attractive, as well as the emanative or *outgoing* power of love, HAS ITS LAWS. And some of these laws I shall proceed now to enumerate.

FIRST. The first law of love, in its attractive form, is this: *the attractive power of love will be in proportion to its emanative power.* In other words, he whose heart goes forth most fully and fervently for the good of others, will most full attract hearts to himself. Love, in its pure state, begets love; and begets it in a proportion or degree corresponding to its own strength. He who blesses others most, will be most blessed in return.

SECOND. Another law of love, in its attractive form, is this. Of loving or holy beings, those *have the most attractive power, who have the greatest capacity of loving.* It is reasonable to suppose, (and the supposition seems to be sustained by the Scriptures,) that there are circles, orders, or spheres of holy beings, rising one above another, and occupying their appropriate positions from man to the Deity, and the sphere that stands in advance of others, has, in consequence of the greater capacities of love which are there enjoyed, a wider and more powerful attractive influence. As angels and seraphs can love more than man, in consequence of their greater capacity of loving, so will they shine out and become radiant with a greater degree of moral beauty, and will therefore have the greater attractive power over others.

THIRD. A third law, which modifies the action of the two preceding, is this: the degree of attracting influence *will depend, in part, on the nature of the being who is subject of attraction.* It is holy beings who are attracted by the beauty of holiness, and not those who are in their sins. And the reason is, that holy beings can see and appreciate the radiance and excellence of holiness; while unholy beings, whose inward life, in being selfishness, is just the opposite of holy love, are *blind.* Having no eye to see the beauty of holiness, they have no heart to feel its power.

FOURTH. It follows from what has been said, that God, the central principle or life of whose existence is love, and whose capacity of loving is infinite, is, by the law of his nature, the *infinite centre of attraction.* It is by the law of love, and not by the pressure of commands and penalties — by the sweet and noble influences of attraction, and not by the goads of compulsion—that he turns and unites the universe of holy beings to himself.

FIFTH. Men feel the influence of divine attraction—the influence of the ineffable beauty of divine love in sweetly drawing them to what is true, and right, and good—just in proportion as they themselves are sanctified. In the beginning of the divine life, when the soul just begins to open its eye upon the beauty of moral excellence, it feels this attractive influence only in a small degree. At that period, the soul, though not exclusively, is kept, in a considerable degree, in a right position, by means of commands, penalties, threats. As it gradually throws off its own selfishness, and comes more and more into the truth and light, it is governed less by fear and more by love. It is drawn, not driven. It follows the path of the holy, because it loves to. All that is necessary, in order to follow the divine voice, is to hear it. "My sheep," says the Saviour, "hear my voice; and I know them; and they follow me." John x. 27.

SIXTH. When the repulsion of sin ceases in the heart, and it experiences assurance of faith and perfection of love, it enters into full harmony with God, and becomes one with him, because, becoming in all things the subject of that divine attraction which draws it to the central source of life, it necessarily ceases to be the subject of any and all separating influences. And as the soul expands in capacity, it becomes the more capable of receiving the divine attraction, and does in fact experience a higher degree of such attraction, and thus passes onward and upward from one degree of heavenly existence to another, from one flaming hierarchy of intelligence and love to another; always advancing, but never reaching; always full, but always expanding; always in unity with God, but never identical with him.

SEVENTH. When the laws of love, in the two forms of emanation and attraction, are in full force, everything in the moral world will be found to be in perfect adjustment.

Every want will be supplied; every duty will be fulfilled; every exigency will be met; every fear will be quieted; every hope will be realized. Truth will correspond to truth; love will harmonize with love; hearts, without losing their true position, will be bound together by the golden tie of divine relationships, and all will be in harmony and peace.

I could say much more upon this interesting and important subject, but must leave it for the present. It is believed that the experience of Christians, whose hearts are closely united with God, will be found to correspond to what has now been said.

PERSONAL FEELINGS

I.

FLOWERS have no tongues, and therefore have no outward speech; but I think they may be said to speak with the heart; and sometimes they utter or suggest thoughts, and enter into little affectionate conversations, which are quite interesting. Some of the weary hours which were occupied in traversing the peninsula of Sinai, were relieved by these little soliloquies. Allow me to give you an instance.

> One day in the desert
>> With pleasure I spied
> A flower in its beauty
>> Looking up at my side.
> And I said, Oh sweet flowret,
>> That bloomest alone,
> What's the worth of thy beauty,
>> Thus shining unknown?

But the flower gave me answer,
　With a smile quite divine,
'Tis the nature, O stranger!
　Of beauty to shine.
Take all I can give thee,
　And when thou art gone,
The light that is in me,
　Will keep shining on.

And, oh gentle stranger,
　Permit me to say,
To keep up thy spirits
　Along this lone way,
While thy heart shall flow outward
　To gladden and bless,
To fount at its centre
　Will never grow less.

I was struck with its answer,
　And left it to glow
To the clear sky above it
　And the pale sands below;
Above and around it
　Its light to impart,
But never exhausting
　The fount at is heart.

II.

AT a little distance from me I noticed the traditionary place where the Saviour is said to have wept over Jerusalem. Reaching the foot of the mountain, I stopped at the garden of Gethsemane. At a little distance on my right was the beautiful chapel and the sepulchre of the Virgin Mary. The traditionary belief is that the dust of the mother reposes near the garden which witnessed the heavy trials of her divine Son. The garden of Gethsemane is now enclosed by a high wall, which overlooks the channel of the Kedron. I entered it, and walked among the flowers, which the hand of Christian veneration loves to cultivate on its sacred soil, and beneath the shade of the aged olive trees, the growth of many hundred — perhaps of a thousand years.

And this, I said to myself, was the garden of preparatory suffering; — the sad and memorable scene of one of the most trying periods of the Saviour's life. This was the place of agony. It was here he kneeled and prayed. "If it be possible, let this cup pass from me. Nevertheless, not as I will, but as Thou wilt."

The world of spirits took an interest in this great struggle. An angel appeared — strengthening him. His prayer was answered. The will of his Father was accomplished. The Son of God was betrayed into the hands of wicked men. His blood flowed upon Calvary. Jerusalem was destroyed. But a world was redeemed.

WRITTEN ON VISITING THE GARDEN OF GETHSEMANE, MAY, 1853.

Oh let me not forget! 'Twas here,
    Earth of the Saviour's grief and toil!
He knelt; — and oft the falling tear
    Mingled his sorrows with thy soil; —
When, in the garden's fearful hour,
He felt the great temptation's power.

Here was the proffered bitter cup.
    "THY WILL BE DONE," the Saviour said.
His faith received, and drank it up;
    Amazed, the baffled tempter fled —
Repulsed, with all his hate and skill,
Before an acquiescent will.

> Oh man! in memory of that hour,
>   Let rising murmurs be repress'd;
> And learn the secret of thy power
>   Within a calm and patient breast.
> "THY WILL BE DONE!" 'Tis that, which rolls
> Their agony from suffering souls.

> Such is the lesson that I find,
>   Here, in the Saviour's place of tears;—
> The lesson, that the trusting mind
>   Has strength to conquer griefs and fears;
> And doomed upon the cross to die,
> Finds death itself a victory.

III.

IT was here, when there was a great tempest, and the ship was covered with the waves, that "he arose and rebuked the winds and the sea, and there was a great calm." And it was probably upon one of the heights rising above these waters, (an old tradition says upon Tell Hattin,) that he uttered those remarkable sayings—without precedent in the annals of mere human thought and wisdom—which constitute the Sermon on the Mount.

At evening I stood at the door of our tent. The stars began to show themselves again. The lake was at a little distance. I heard its gentle voice. Excepting the sound of the waters, there was silence on the plain and on the mountains. One feeling occupied my heart. One thought subordinated all others.

> Strange is the deep, mysterious tie
> Which makes departed ages nigh;
> But God has formed it; and its power
> Has marked with me this sacred hour.
> 'Twas thus, I thought, as thy bright sea,

Blue-tinted wave of Galilee!
With gentle sound and motion sank
Upon the bold and rocky bank.

Oh, Lake and Land—where memories last—
Which link the present with the past;
Whose waves and rocky heights restore
Departed scenes and forms once more!
'Twas *here* He pressed the conscious earth;—
'Twas *here* his heavenly thoughts had birth.
Oh give me back, if yet ye can,
This "Son of God," this "Son of man."

He comes;—he walks upon the sea;—
"Have faith," he says, *"and walk with me."*
I go—I sink—he takes my hand;
I, too, upon the waters stand;—
But soon from cliff and mountain side
The tempest sweeps the foaming tide;
The lightnings flash;—the billows rise;—
Storms lift and dash them to the skies.

'Twas to the weak his hand he gave;
And has he power the weak to save?
Fierce and more fierce the billows roll,
But FAITH has anchored in the soul.
Amid the clouds I see his form;
I hear his voice amid the storm;
The tempest listens to his will;
The winds are hushed;—the waves are still.

IV.

I wanted repose; and I found it in the desert. I wanted
communion with God; and I found it there. I found it
in the day, in the vastness of its objects, and its silence. I found it still more in the night, when magni-

tude enlarges itself, and silence becomes more silent.
I found it in the earth beneath, and in the heavens
above. Often I watched the stars. Beautiful as the
heavenly mansions, they looked out from their blue
abodes—clear and lovely—as if they were eyes of
that great Being who fills their urns with light. There
was one with its large angelic eye that came with
peculiar sweetness. It danced upon the mountain
tops. It had no audible utterance; but there was a
divine language in its smile, which spake of heavenly peace. It was in the desert of Sinai that I gave it
a place in my memory. It was in the vast wilderness,
which had inspired the prophetic impulses and the
songs of Moses, that I watched the mild splendour
of its beams, and endeavoured to record the emotions
excited by its mysterious but lovely presence.

WRITTEN IN THE WILDERNESS OF SINAI.

I marked the bright, the silver star,
    That nightly decked our desert way,
As shining from its depths afar,
    Its heavenly radiance seemed to say;—
Oh look! from mists and shadows clear,
My cheering light is always here.

I saw thee. And at once I knew,
    Star of the desert, in my heart;—
That thou didst shine, the emblem true
    Of that bright star, whose beams impart,
From night to night, from day to day,
The solace of their inward ray.

There is a beam to light the mind;
    There is a star the soul to cheer;
And they, that heavenly light who find,
    Shall always see it burning clear;

The same its bright, celestial face,
In every change of time and place.

Star of my heart! that long hast shone,
    To cheer the inward spirit's sky,
Illumin'd from the heavenly throne,
    Thou hast a ray that cannot die.
'Tis God that lights thee. And with Him
No sky is dark; no star is dim.

Religious Stanzas

Penitence.

Oh, say when errors oft and black
   Have deeply stained the inmost soul,
Who then shall call the wanderer back,
   Who make the broken spirit whole?
Who give the tortured and depressed
The grateful balm, that soothes to rest?

When storms are driven across the sky,
   The rainbow decks the troubled clouds,
And there is One whose love is nigh,
   Where grief annoys and darkness shrouds;
He'll stretch abroad his bow of peace,
And bid the storm and tempest cease.

Then go, vain world, 'tis time to part,
   Too long and darkly hast thou twined
Around this frail, corrupted heart,
   And poisoned the immortal mind;
Oh, I have known the pangs that spring
From pleasure's beak and folly's sting.

Hail, Prince of Heaven! Hail, Bow of rest!
    Oh, downward scatter mercy's ray,
And all the darkness of my breast
    Shall quickly turn to golden day.
With Thee is peace; no griefs annoy;
And tears are grateful gems of joy.

If There is Sunshine in the Face.

If there is sunshine in the face,
    And joy upon the brow,
Do not suppose, that there's a trace
    Of answering joy below.

And what avails the outward light,
    Upon the face the smile;
If all within is dark as night,
    If all is dead the while.

Deep in the heart the evil lies,
    Which nought on earth can cure,
Aversion to the only Wise,
    To God, the only Pure.

Oh Thou, who giv'st the heart renewed,
    Withhold it not from me,
That, all my enmity subdued,
    I may rejoice in Thee.

Thou Giver of the Rising Light

Thou Giver of the rising light,
    Thou Author of the morning ray;
At whose command the shades of night
    Are changed to bright and sudden day;

Thou too canst rend the clouded heart,
   Enveloped in the shades of sin;
And let the light that dwelt apart,
   The glory and the gladness in.

Oh God, our Father and our Friend,
   Dark is the cloud that wraps us now;
But not in vain our prayers ascend,
   Nor hopeless at thy feet we bow.
'Tis in the dark, distressing hour,
   That thou dost hear thy people's cry;
And come and clothe them in thy power,
   And hide them in thy majesty.

LONG DID THE CLOUDS AND DARKNESS ROLL.

LONG did the clouds and darkness roll
   Around my troubled breast;
No starlight shone upon my soul,
   My footsteps found no rest.

To human help I looked around,
   But vainly sought relief;
No balm of Gilead I found,
   No healing for my grief.

Then to the Saviour's help I cried;
   He listening heard my prayer;
I saw his wounded hands and side,
   And felt that hope was there.
He guides me in the better way;
   He makes my footsteps strong;
The gloomy night is changed to day,
   And sadness changed to song.

THE FIRST DAY OF THE NEW LIFE.

"AH, how long shall I delight
  In the memory of that day,"
When the shades of mental night
  Sudden passed away!

Long around my darkened view
  Had those lingering shadows twined;
Till the Gospel, breaking through,
  Chased them from my mind.

There was light in everything,
  Every thing was bathed in bliss;
Trees did wave, and birds did sing,
  Full of happiness.

Beauty in the woods shone forth,
  Beauty did the flowers display;
And my glorious Maker's worth
  Beamed with matchless ray.

"Ah, how long shall I delight
  In the memory of that day,"
When the shades of mental night
  Sudden passed away.

JEHOVAH, SOVEREIGN OF MY HEART.

JEHOVAH, Sov'reign of my heart!
  My joy by night and day!
From Thee, oh may I never part,
  From thee, ne'er go astray.

Whene'er allurements round me stand,
　And tempt me from my choice;
Oh, let me find thy gracious hand,
　Oh, let me hear thy voice.

This vain and feeble heart, I know,
　To worldly ways is prone;
But penitential tears shall show,
　There's joy in Thee alone.
With God all darkness turns to day;
　With Him all sorrows flee;
Thou art the true and living way,
　And I will walk in Thee.

Man's Spirit Hath an Upward Look

Man's spirit hath an upward look,
　And robes itself with heavenly wings;
E'en when 'tis here compelled to brook
　Confinement to terrestrial things.

Its eye is fastened on the skies;
　Its wings for flight are opened wide;
Why doth it hesitate to rise?
　And still upon the earth abide;

And would'st thou seek the cause to know,
　And never more its course repress;
Then from those wings their burden throw,
　And set them free from worldliness.
Shake off the earthly cares that stay
　Their energy and upward flight;
And thou shalt see them make their way
　To joy, and liberty, and light.

ALTHOUGH AFFLICTION SMITES MY HEART

ALTHOUGH affliction smites my heart,
    And earthly pleasures flee,
There is one bliss that ne'er shall part,
    My joy, oh God, in Thee.

That joy is like the orb of day,
    When clouds its track pursue;
The shades and darkness throng its way,
    But sunlight struggles through.

Oh Thou, my everlasting light,
    On whom my hopes rely;
With Thee the darkest path is bright,
    And fears and sorrows die.

IF CLOUDS ARISE AND STORMS APPEAR.

IF clouds arise and storms appear,
    If fortune, friends, and all forsake me,
There's One to shed with mine the tear,
    And to his bleeding bosom take me.

Blest Saviour! Let it be my lot,
    To tread with Thee this round of being;
Thy love and mercy alter not,
    When every sunbeam friend is fleeing.

Oh, be it thine to guide my soul
    Along the wave of life's dark ocean;
And nought I'll fear, when billows roll,
    Nor dread the whirlwind's rude commotion.

Thy love shall be my polar light,
    And whether weal or woe betide me,

Through raging storm and shadowy night,
  Its blaze shall shine to cheer and guide me.

THE DIVINE LIFE.

OH, sacred union with the Perfect Mind!
  Transcendent bliss, which Thou alone canst give!
How blest are they, this pearl of price who find,
  And dead to earth, have learnt in Thee to live.

Thus, in thine arms of love, oh God, I lie,
  Lost, and forever lost, to all but Thee.
My happy soul, since it hath learnt to die,
  Hath found new life in thine Infinity.

Oh, go and learn this lesson of the cross;
  And tread the way which saints and prophets trod,
Who, counting life, and self, and all things loss,
  Have found in inward death the life of God.